SUSPICIOUS CIRCUMSTANCES

BLITZ EDITIONS

Published by Blitz Editions
an imprint of Bookmart Ltd
Registered Number 2372865
Trading as Bookmart Ltd, Desford Road, Enderby
Leicester LE9 5AD

This book was produced
by Amazon Publishing Ltd

Cover design: Peter Dolton
Text design: Jim Reader
Production Manager: Sue Gray
Editorial Manager: Roz Williams

Printed in the Slovak Republic
51736

ISBN 1 85605 203 6

This material has previously appeared in *Fated Destiny*.

Every effort has been made to contact the copyright holders for the pictures.
In some cases they have been untraceable, for which we offer our apologies.
Thanks to the Hulton Deutsch Collection Ltd, who supplied most of them.
Pictures have been provided as follows: Ancient Art and Architecture Collection (pp 15 top, 18 bottom, 19, 22, 24–27), Fortean Picture Library (p 17 top), Fotomas Index (p 24 top), Hulton Deutsch Collection Ltd (pp 2, 5–11 bottom, 12, 13 bottom, 16 top, 21 top, 28, 30–33, 35, 38, 39, 41, 42, 46, 48 bottom, 49–51 top, 52 bottom, 55 bottom, 56, 57, 62, 64, 74–77, 80), Mary Evans Picture Library (pp 14, 15 bottom, 16 bottom, 17 bottom, 18 top, 60, 61, 63, 66, 67, 69, 70, 72), Peter Newark's American Pictures (p 54), Peter Newark's Historical Pictures (p 45), Peter Newark's Western Americana (pp 20, 21 bottom, 23, 79), Popperfoto (pp 3 bottom, 47), Rex Features Ltd (pp 3 top, 4, 13 top, 48 top), Roger Viollet (pp 40, 43, 44), Syndication International (pp 51 bottom, 59, 65, 73), Topham Picture Source (p 11 top).

Cover: All pictures including the back cover supplied by the Hulton Deutsch Collection Ltd.

The Authors

Karen Farrington is a journalist who has worked for both national newspapers, and as freelance, for the best selling weekly women's magazines. Her broad experience has brought her into contact with some of the most intriguing mysteries, compelling crimes and moving animal stories of recent times.

Nick Constable, also a journalist, has spent many years working in Fleet Street and covered top stories including the famine of Ethiopia, the government-backed assassinations of street children in Brazil and the Gulf War. He has also worked extensively to expose cruelty to animals in Britain and around the world.

SUSPICIOUS CIRCUMSTANCES

MARILYN MONROE
The murder of a myth

Marilyn Monroe was an insatiable sex goddess whose only crime was the desire to make men happy. In the end, it seemed, that was at the cost of her own happiness ...

Dr Ralph Greenson was first to inspect the body. He had broken a pane of glass to enter her bedroom but he knew she was dead even before he reached her side. She was lying face down, sprawled naked across her bed. In her right hand she still gripped her bedside telephone. 'I could see from many feet away that she was no longer living,' he said. 'It looked as if she was trying to make a phone call before she was overwhelmed.'

It was just before dawn on Sunday 5 August 1962, and Marilyn Monroe, the greatest sex goddess the world has ever known, was dead.

The years since have not dimmed her legend. Indeed, it has been fuelled, if not enhanced, by revelations of promiscuous exploits, scandalous affairs, marital infidelities and sinister intrigue.

The luscious, ripe peach of a girl with a walk that spoke volumes and lips that men lusted for had enjoyed countless lovers. Among them were stars and politicians – including US president Jack Kennedy and his brother Robert, the attorney general. She was beloved by millions. Yet she died alone. The question is: Did she die by her own hand? Or was she murdered?

Decades later, the life and death of Marilyn Monroe remains one of the most eerily fascinating mysteries, linking the murky worlds of crime, politics and Hollywood ...

UNLOVED AND UNWANTED

The girl the world came to know as Marilyn Monroe was born Norma Jean Mortensen at Los Angeles General Hospital on 1 June 1926. Her mother Gladys, an emotionally disturbed film cutter, appeared on the birth certificate under her maiden name, Gladys Monroe. Her father was listed as Martin Edward

Left: ***Baby Norma Jean Mortensen, who grew up to have the world's most famous face.***

Opposite: ***A screen goddess and dream centrefold, Marilyn was adored by millions.***

Below: ***Initially Marilyn found success as a model with brunette hair. But she soon discovered 'gentlemen prefer blondes'.***

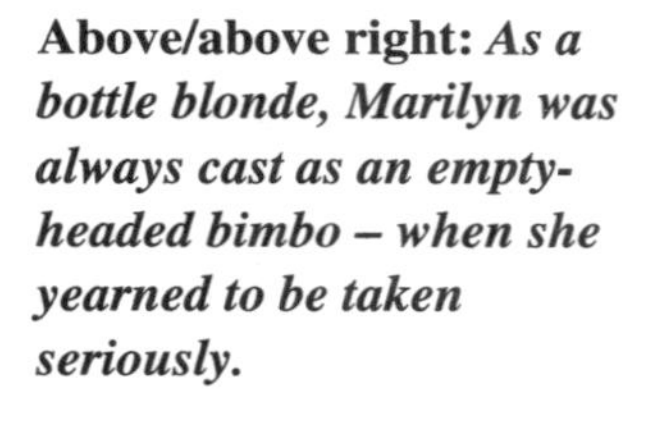

Above/above right: ***As a bottle blonde, Marilyn was always cast as an empty-headed bimbo – when she yearned to be taken seriously.***

STARVED OF LOVE AND SEDUCED AT 15 BY HER FOSTER FATHER, THE POOR GIRL WAS OVERJOYED TO FIND HERSELF PREGNANT.

Mortensen. The young Marilyn, however, grew up never knowing who her real father was. Her mother's first husband, Jack Baker, had left her in 1923. She had then married Mortensen, a Danish baker, but the two parted before Norma Jean's birth. He was later killed in a motorcycle accident. The girl's most likely father was Charles Stanley Gifford, her mother's boss at the film cutting laboratory. After his brief fling with Gladys, Gifford left to start a dairy farm near Los Angeles. Remarried, he kept Marilyn's existence a secret from his new family until a deathbed confession in 1965.

Only two weeks after Marilyn's birth, her mother was committed to an asylum after trying to slit a friend's throat. Although Gladys continued to visit her daughter from time to time, Marilyn spent the next 15 years in children's homes and with a succession of foster parents. Shuttled from home to home, she became a shy, nervous girl who panicked easily.

At the age of 11 she went to live with her aunt, Grace McKee, and was enrolled at Van Nuys High School. It was here, she later said, that she first had sex, with a fellow student. Despite becoming her legal guardian, Grace McKee continued to foster out her charge, and at the age of 15 Marilyn was seduced by one of her foster fathers. The poor girl was overjoyed to find herself pregnant but her aunt was horrified. Some stories have it that the child was aborted; others that Marilyn gave birth to a baby boy and that it was adopted. A friend quoted Marilyn as saying: 'It was like being kicked in the head. I begged them not to take my baby away, but they said it was the best thing. They said I was too young to take care of him.'

Aunt Grace wanted Marilyn off her hands, and in 1942 she was pushed into her first marriage, to boy-next-door Jim Dougherty, a 21-year-old night shift worker at an aircraft factory. The life of a working-class housewife soon bored her, and escape came when Dougherty was conscripted in World War 2. They lived for a while on a base in California where she killed time in bars.

Marilyn soon discovered that she could make money by letting men take her back to their hotel rooms. As she told her maid Lena Pepitone many years later: 'I let my husband Jim do whatever he wanted with me even though I didn't really love him. So what was the difference?'

NUDE MODELLING

After Jim was posted abroad, Marilyn signed herself on at the Blue Book Model Agency and started posing for magazines and calendars. A natural brunette, she soon discovered that gentlemen preferred blondes. She went further than her famous bleached hairstyle, however. She also peroxided her pubic hair – a painful process but, she believed, essential if she was to wear sheer white dresses and no underwear!

As a model, Marilyn had no qualms about posing nude, but friends dismiss stories that she starred in pornographic films. Her famous calendar shot, lying naked on red velvet, was tame by today's standards. (Studio bosses were later so horrified by it that they ordered her to deny having posed for it at all. She refused and told everyone she had done it to pay the rent.)

Los Angeles was a city of dreams, and it was almost inevitable that Marilyn should meet an agent who would advise her to use her powers of seduction to become a movie star. With Dougherty now divorced and forgotten along with the rest of her tormented past, Marilyn sought invitations to Hollywood parties where she met the big studio moguls to whom she distributed her favours freely. Among them was Twentieth-Century Fox founder Joe Schenk, who was 70 and asked only that she sat with him in the nude while he fondled her breasts. Another of her lovers was Columbia boss Harry Cohn who, according to Marilyn, would indulge in no conversation apart from the simple instruction: 'Get into bed'.

In her desperate bid for fame, she later told Lena, she would have slept with almost anybody so long as they were 'nice'. She said: 'If I made them happy, why not? It didn't hurt. I like to see men smile.'

Her first steps up the ladder of stardom came with a string of minor parts in long-faded films like *Ladies of the Chorus*. But she came to the notice of the movie fans when she took the stereotyped role of a dumb blonde in the film *Asphalt Jungle*. The producer who gave her the role, Arthur Hornblow Junior, said: 'She arrived on the set scared to death and dressed as a cheap tart. But she had a quality that touched the heart, evoked tenderness, made the blood race and stirred the senses. This can only be found in a juvenile delinquent!' Fellow producer Billy Wilder said: 'She had breasts like granite and a brain like cheese.'

Suddenly the poor girl from the wrong side of the tracks was sought after at smart cocktail parties – and at less salubrious Hollywood grope-and-groan shindigs. Being blonde, bosomy and deliciously beautiful, Marilyn was pigeon-holed into the dumb blonde category in real life as well as on set. Yet the actress was far from dumb and craved intelligent conversation.

She may even have sought an affair with the genius Einstein. Actress Shelley Winters recalled Marilyn telling her that she fancied him. When Shelley laughed at her notion of an affair with the most famous scientist and mathematician of the

'SHE HAD BREASTS LIKE GRANITE AND A BRAIN LIKE CHEESE.'

Below: ***Among her celebrated Hollywood co-stars was brooding idol Humphrey Bogart, who was even more sultry than she was.***

Above: ***Taking a break from filming, Marilyn showed she was a girl who wanted to have fun.***

Right: ***Loving and giving, Marilyn was every man's ideal girl. She enjoyed making men happy – and it showed.***

Below: ***Baseball star Joe diMaggio hated his bride's sexy image and refused to take part in the Hollywood circus that dogged her every step.***

century, and an old man besides, Marilyn replied: 'That has nothing to do with it. Anyway, I hear he's very young for his age.' (After her death, a large framed photograph of Einstein was found among her possessions. On it was written: 'To Marilyn, with love and thanks, Albert Einstein.')

FRUSTRATED SEX SYMBOL

By the early fifties, Marilyn Monroe was stuck with the 'dumb blonde' image that coloured not only her locks but her life. She craved the care, affection and respect that no man had yet given her. At a party she met Joe diMaggio, the greatest baseball player the game had ever known, an authentic American hero. He was also a good man. They married in January 1954.

At 37, diMaggio was 12 years Marilyn's senior, and he put a protective shield around his new beautiful bride. He loathed her 'sex goddess' image, however, and reckoned the only place she should be sexy was at home with him. He refused to accompany her to showbusiness parties and shunned publicity shots with her. He was a homebird. Marilyn, now hooked on fame and under intense pressure from the studios, could not accept the role of a submissive housewife. They divorced only nine months after the wedding.

Marilyn was bitter. 'What good is being a sex symbol if it drives your man away?' she complained.

The movie star's next marriage was equally sensational. While still with diMaggio, she had been carrying a torch for playwright Arthur Miller. In June 1956, after Marilyn had divorced her second husband and Miller had divorced his first wife, the two were wed. By marrying the playwright, Marilyn was proving an important point to herself. She was no dumb blonde – she was the wife of one of America's most renowned intellectuals. She told the world: 'I've never loved anyone as much as I love Arthur.'

Her happiness was short-lived, however. Miller tried to provide for his wife a settled and ordered home life, but the attempt, in his words, to 'balance the two disjointed worlds' in which they lived became too difficult. Miller's work schedule prevented the couple wining, dining and partying in the manner Marilyn (and her studio bosses) had come to expect. The writer was soon spending little time with his beautiful wife, shutting himself away in his study and working all day and late into the evening.

Often Marilyn would dress and make up ready for a dinner or a show, only to be disappointed when Miller would call off the date, claiming to be too busy. Sobbing with rage and disappointment, Marilyn would rip off her clothes and go to bed alone.

Marilyn's greatest disappointment, however, was in her attempts to have a longed-for child by Miller. Soon after her marriage she became pregnant but had a miscarriage after the sixth week. When her next pregnancy ended the same way she was beside herself with grief, sobbing: 'I can never have kids again.'

The star and the writer drifted further apart. Marilyn looked for love elsewhere, and fell for French actor Yves Montand, her co-star in the movie *Let's Make Love*. Their brief affair flourished during the filming, when Miller was away in Ireland and Montand's wife Simone Signoret was at home in Paris. Marilyn hoped their affair would lead to marriage but, filming over, Montand thanked her for a 'nice time' and flew straight back to his wife. Marilyn was left sobbing among the flowers and unopened champagne bottles in a hotel room she had booked for a romantic farewell.

Marilyn tried to drown her misery with booze, pills and a succession of affairs. Her marriage to Miller came to an end during the making of *The Misfits*, which he wrote. Her blazing rows with him on set were blamed for the death of co-star Clarke Gable a day after filming ended. Monroe and Miller flew home on different planes and she announced to a New York columnist that she was divorcing.

Above: ***Marilyn thought marriage to playwright Arthur Miller would bring her the credibility she craved. In fact it brought her only misery.***

The actress still clung blindly to the hope of a reconciliation with Yves Montand. A meeting was planned in New York at Christmas 1960, but just days before Simone Signoret telephoned Marilyn begging her to keep away from her husband. Montand cancelled the trip at the last minute.

ANY MAN WAS FAIR GAME FOR THE FRUSTRATED SEX SYMBOL: SHE SEDUCED POLITICIANS AND SHE SEDUCED HER PLUMBER.

At this desperate point in her life, with her marriage in ruins and rejected by her French lover, Marilyn turned back to Joe diMaggio for consolation. When he wasn't around, it was champagne, pills and a string of lovers, from politicians to a plumber working in her apartment block. Any available man was fair game for the insatiable love goddess. She hired a handsome masseur and seduced him at one of their afternoon sessions. She would invite her chauffeur to her room and lock the door for several hours.

She told one of her lovers, young screenwriter Hans Lembourne, who later became a Danish MP: 'I don't know whether I'm good or bad in bed. I can't sustain loving relationships. I drink, I lie. I often want to die – though I'm deadly scared of death. I

Left: ***In 1960 Marilyn starred in* Let's Make Love, *written by Miller, opposite Frenchman Yves Montand, one of her many amours. The film set was fraught with difficulties and marked the end of her marriage.***

believe in marriage and faithfulness, yet I go to bed with others when I'm married. God help me, what a mess.'

Significantly, she admitted to Lembourne that she was terrified of ending her days in an asylum, like her mother (and indeed her grandparents long before). 'I resemble my mother,' she confessed. 'I'm afraid I'll go mad like her.'

In her book *Marilyn Monroe Confidential*, Lena Pepitone recorded her impressions of the star when she was interviewed by her for the job as her maid. Although Lena grew extremely fond of her boss, she was horrified by her appearance at that first meeting.

The star was totally nude, as was often her habit as she wandered around her Los Angeles home. Said Lena: 'Her blonde hair looked unwashed, and was a mess. I was astonished by the way she smelled. She needed a bath, badly. Without make-up she was pale and tired looking. Her celebrated figure seemed more overweight than voluptuous. As she sprawled on a white couch she brought to mind a deluxe prostitute after a busy night in a plush brothel.'

However, Marilyn would go to extreme lengths to look good for special occasions. One such was a date with Frank Sinatra during a fling with the singer which she hoped would lead to marriage. Lena Pepitone realised the closeness of their relationship when she saw Sinatra 'slip two gorgeous emerald earrings on Marilyn's ears ... they then kissed so passionately that I was embarrassed to be standing nearby.'

Frank Sinatra did not have marriage in mind, however. He was having affairs with other women and did not want any publicity. He even insisted Marilyn keep out of sight when she was staying at his home. One evening, slightly tipsy after drinking champagne while waiting for him in the bedroom, the actress wandered nude into the room where Sinatra and his friends were playing poker. Furious, he hissed: 'Get your fat ass upstairs!'

Sinatra eventually dropped Marilyn in favour of dancer Juliet Prowse, and the movie star sunk back into her heavy-drinking, pill-popping, sluttish ways at home in Los Angeles. Lena Pepitone recalled how the star would gnaw the meat off a bone, then drop it on the bedclothes, wiping her greasy hands on the sheets.

Right: ***Jack Kennedy, US president and philanderer, who bedded Marilyn before passing her on to his brother Robert.***

Below: ***Marilyn adopted this hallmark pose in the 1955 film* The Seven Year Itch.**

THE PRESIDENT ENLIVENED THE BORING OFFICIAL FUNCTIONS BY PUTTING HIS HAND UP HER SKIRT AT THE DINNER TABLE.

Left: *Marilyn and Montgomery Clift arrive for the preview of* **The Misfits** *in 1960. A month later she went into a psychiatric hospital for treatment after suffering serious bouts of depression.*

PRESIDENTIAL PHILANDERER

The date 20 January 1961 was an important one in the life of Marilyn Monroe. Her divorce from Arthur Miller was finalized and John F. Kennedy was inaugurated as president of the USA. Marilyn already knew the handsome young Democratic senator from Massachusetts very well indeed ...

Jack Kennedy was an astonishing philanderer. It is amazing that word of his affairs did not leak to a wider audience during the president's lifetime. But the fierce loyalty of his entire White House staff meant that he would be alerted about his wife's movements and given due warning as to when there was need to break up a sex session or even a full-scale drug orgy. His philandering was also facilitated by his friendship with Peter Lawford. Actor Lawford was JFK's brother-in-law (he had married Jack's sister Pat) and he lived in Santa Monica, California, where his beachfront home was headquarters for both Jack and brother Bobby's West Coast expeditions.

It was here that the two were introduced to the world's most famous movie star, Marilyn Monroe. It is generally believed that both brothers had affairs with Marilyn and that they treated her cynically and dropped her harshly.

She was by this time dreadfully unstable, and even to have encouraged her into a clandestine friendship would have been cruel beyond belief. Yet they did just that – with tragic consequences.

Lawford, whom Marilyn had long known through his 'Rat Pack' fellowship with Frank Sinatra, arranged many meetings between JFK and Monroe. When Kennedy won the Democratic presidential nomination he made a barnstorming acceptance speech at the Los Angeles Coliseum, with Marilyn cheering him on. She then joined the young Kennedy for a skinny-dipping party at Lawford's beach house. Kennedy suddenly decided to stay on in California one extra day.

After JFK became president in January 1961, Marilyn sometimes travelled with him in disguise on the presidential jet Air Force One. At private parties Kennedy used to pinch and squeeze her and tell her dirty jokes. He was fond of putting his hand up her skirt at the dinner table. One night he kept going until he discovered she wasn't wearing panties. He took his hand away fast. 'He hadn't counted on going that far,' Marilyn joked.

In May 1962 Jack Kennedy held his 45th birthday party in Madison Square Garden. Marilyn was there at his side. She waddled onto the stage in a skin-tight dress and managed to blurt out a few lines of 'Happy Birthday'. She was scared and drunk. The crowd did not notice but JFK did. Marilyn Monroe could become an embarrassment. She would have to go.

In the last year of her life, the sex goddess was noticing the signs of her age – and she hated them. She said her breasts were getting flabby and she worried about stretch marks on her bust and bottom. 'I can't act,' she told Lena. 'When my face and body go I'll be finished.'

She even stuttered, an affliction the cause of which dated back to her childhood. She told a friend: 'When I was

Below: *Emerging from hospital, Marilyn was apparently cured of the drink and drugs addiction that caused her mood swings.*

Above: ***Attorney General Robert Kennedy was supposed to be attending a dinner party on the night Marilyn died. He never showed up.***

nine a man forced me to do something. I've never got over it and now I stutter when I'm angry or upset.'

Her film career was in tatters and she rarely turned up on the set on scheduled filming days. She fell into deep bouts of depression, possibly made a failed suicide bid and claimed that she had procured yet another abortion (that would make no fewer than 14).

Marilyn's last picture was calle *Something's Got to Give* – and so ethi did. Taking more pills than ever, sl e oft did not arrive on the set until the af ernoo Sometimes she did not turn up at ll. H co-star Dean Martin quit and she w s fire The film was abandoned.

Poor Marilyn turned more and mo e to t Kennedy clan for support. She ha shar her bed with the president and had th n be passed on by him to his brother Robe t. Th had both enjoyed the sexual favour of t most lusted-after woman on Ear h. Y neither wanted anything more to do ith h Her life-style had become an acu embarrassment to them as, at the ag of 3 with a long history of psychiatric pr blem she turned more and more to drugs.

The Kennedys realized that, w th h diaries and her knowledge o the Californian secret partying, the orld most popular blonde might be beli ved she decided to break the presidenti l co of silence. It has been suggested th t wo was passed to Marilyn not to atte npt contact either Bobby or Jack ever ag in.

She was cut from the clan, and it w enough to send the unstable mov e st over the edge.

Right: ***The bed in which Marilyn died. Was it suicide, as the inquest decided, or murder?***

A CONVENIENT DEATH

On the morning of 5 August 1962, Marilyn was found dead in bed at her newly acquired home on Fifth Helena Drive in Brentwood, Los Angeles. Tell-tale empty pill bottles were on the bedside table. Had she died by her own hand? Was it accident or suicide? Or murder?

The inquest verdict that she had killed herself by a barbiturate overdose was not seriously questioned for about nine months. But then, as the shock of her death receded, experts began to analyse the evidence more reasonably and to question the 'convenient' way in which Marilyn's life had been snuffed out.

Officially, the overdose that killed the star was more than 50 sleeping tablets. Marilyn, according to her aides, had great difficulty swallowing tablets without large quantities of water. Police who were called to the house found no glass in the bedroom. A post-mortem showed virtually no fluid in her stomach. And strangely, there was little trace of the drug in the victim's digestive tract.

All this evidence pointed to a frightening new theory: that Marilyn died not

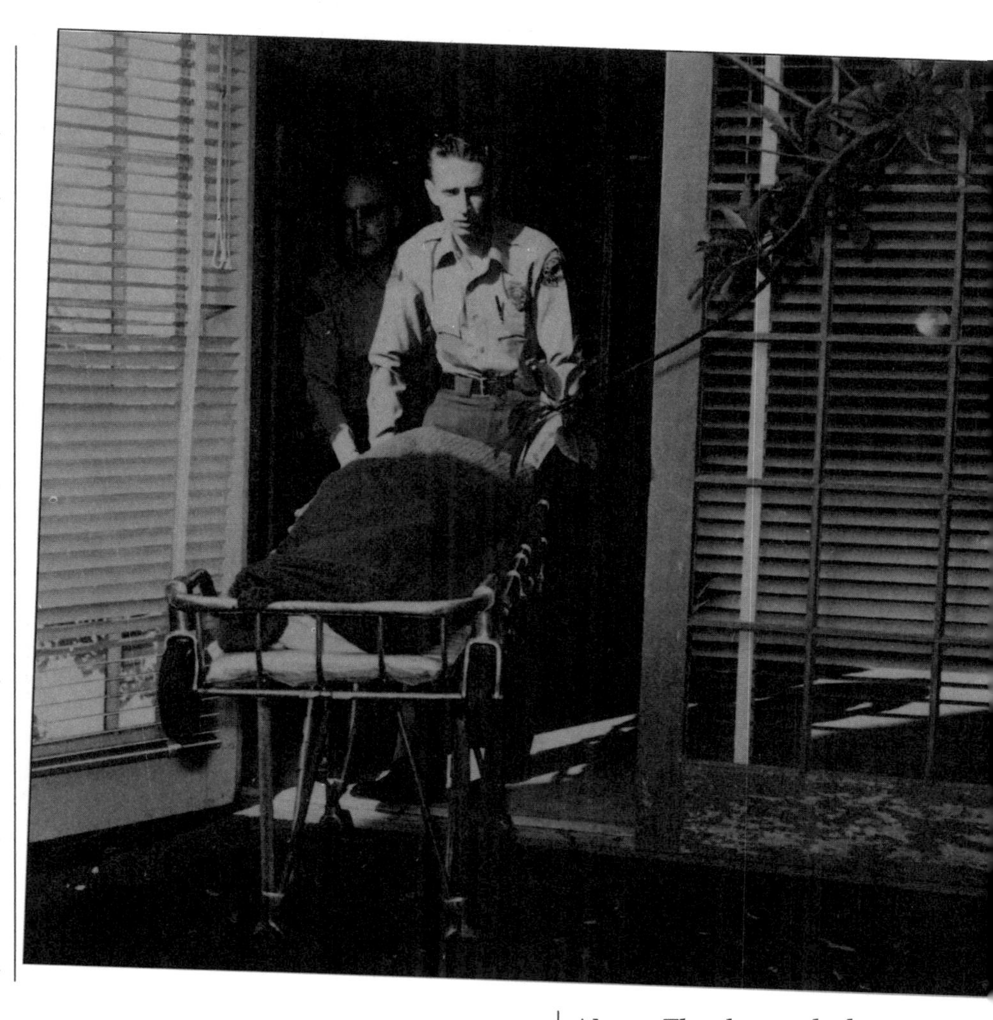

Above: ***The glamour had gone when her body was wheeled out of the house she lived in so briefly, where the pangs of misery she had known grew acute.***

Left: ***Actor Peter Lawford and his wife Pat Kennedy. They introduced J.F.K. to sex queen Marilyn, a meeting which had disastrous consequences for her emotionally.***

Above: ***Jack and Robert Kennedy with FBI chief J. Edgar Hoover. After her death, there was speculation that all three were involved in the cover-up of Marilyn's killing.***

because she had swallowed an overdose of barbiturates but because drugs had been injected into her. Even top pathologists who investigated the case could come up with no other conclusion than that an intruder had injected the deadly barbiturate dose directly into her body.

But why? According to one of her closest friends, Robert Slatzer, Marilyn felt that the Kennedy brothers had used her then abandoned her. Her calls to the White House were no longer being returned and she was out for revenge.

Slatzer said that two important meetings had been planned for the day following her death. One was with her lawyer; the other was a press conference. At this conference, said Slatzer, Marilyn was going to reveal the truth about her love sessions with the president, or with the attorney general, or both.

The only thing that would have stopped her revelations would have been a phone call or a visit from Robert Kennedy on the night of 4 August – her last day on Earth.

On that night a dinner party had been planned at the home of Peter Lawford, down the road in Santa Monica. It was rumoured that Robert Kennedy was due to turn up. He never did. Nor did Marilyn, who at about 8 pm received a phone call from Lawford inquiring if she was about to set out to join him and his wife Pat for the dinner. According to Lawford at the inquest, Marilyn told him she felt too tired and said: 'Say goodbye to Pat and say goodbye to the president, and say goodbye to yourself, because you're such a nice guy.'

'AN OBVIOUS CASE OF MURDER'

There were rumours at the time that Robert Kennedy, staying at the St Francis Hotel, San Francisco, had travelled south to Los Angeles on the night of 4 August for a meeting with Monroe. The story was denied but the theories that Marilyn had been silenced grew stronger.

It was said that her house had been bugged by Robert Kennedy, by the FBI, and even by Jimmy Hoffa, head of the Mafia-linked Teamsters' Union who was seeking incriminating evidence against his arch-enemy, the attorney general.

The theory that the FBI was involved in the star's death is not as far-fetched as it at first sounds. FBI chief J. Edgar Hoover made his agents collect for him every scrap of information about the private lives of leading politicians. It was one of the

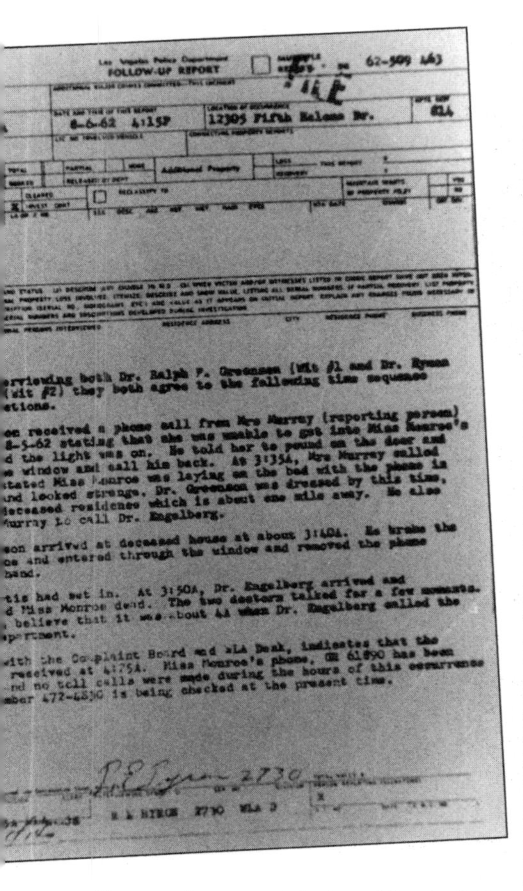

FOLLOW-UP REPORT 62-509 463

8-6-62 4:15P 12305 Fifth Helena Dr.

erviewing both Dr. Ralph R. Greenson (Wit #1 and Dr. Hyman
(Wit #2) they both agree to the following time sequence
etions.

oc received a phone call from Mrs Murray (reporting person)
8-5-62 stating that she was unable to get into Miss Monroe's
d the light was on. He told her to pound on the door and
e window and call him back. At 3:35A, Mrs Murray called
stated Miss Monroe was laying on the bed with the phone in
and looked strange. Dr. Greenson was dressed by this time,
deceased residence which is about one mile away. He also
Murray to call Dr. Engelberg.

son arrived at deceased house at about 3:40A. He broke the
ne and entered through the window and removed the phone
hand.

tis had set in. At 3:50A, Dr. Engelberg arrived and
d Miss Monroe dead. The two doctors talked for a few moments.
believe that it was about 4A when Dr. Engelberg called the
epartment.

with the Complaint Board and WLA Desk, indicates that the
received at 4:25A. Miss Monroe's phone, GR 61890 has been
and no toll calls were made during the hours of this occurrence
mber 472-4830 is being checked at the present time.

R. E. Byron 2730

easons Hoover's eccentric handling of the FBI had previously gone unchallenged. And in the Kennedys' case, the FBI's personal files bulged with scandal. Neither John nor his younger brother had been totally secretive in his extra-marital activities. In their relationships with Marilyn Monroe, it was thought that her state of depression and suspected nervous disorder might indeed cause her to spill the beans and irreparably damage the stature of the presidency.

Another sensational theory arose because of the belief that Monroe had an abortion about this time – and that the baby would have been Bobby Kennedy's. Marilyn had tried to contact him at the Justice Department in Washington on numerous occasions in the weeks before her death. Had an unborn child been the cause of Marilyn's death?

The horrifying storyline that secret agents killed Marilyn to protect the Kennedy brothers from worldwide disgrace was backed up by the research of dozens of authors, including the redoubtable Norman Mailer.

Even the first police officer to arrive on the scene, Sergeant Jack Clemmons, said: 'I was shocked to high heaven by the official verdict of suicide. It was obviously a case of murder.'

A further bizarre twist to the plot was advanced in 1981 by a reformed criminal, Ronald 'Sonny' Gibson. In his book *Mafia Kingpin*, he said that while working for the mobsters he had learned of a unique deal between the FBI and the Mafia. FBI chief J. Edgar Hoover had been furious with Marilyn over her embarrassing affairs with leading politicians and had agreed to turn a blind eye to her removal. The Mafia therefore ordered hitmen to bump off the star in order to repay old favours done for them by the FBI.

Weird theories indeed. But perhaps no more so than the established truth – that the most powerful man in the world and his brother had been having clandestine affairs with the most popular film star ever known.

The questions remain ... Who killed Marilyn Monroe? Did she die by her own hand, by accident or suicide? Or was she murdered?

When poor Marilyn's naked body was examined by her personal physician, Dr Ralph Greenson, she was clutching a telephone. Whom had she been trying to ring?

THE QUESTION WAS BEING ASKED: 'HAD THE PRESIDENT SILENCED THE SHOWGIRL?'

Left: ***A death report made by police detailing the 3.30 am call by housekeeper Mrs Murray to Dr Ralph Greenson when she failed to get a response from Marilyn through a locked bedroom door.***

Below: ***Ex-husband Joe diMaggio made a twice-weekly order 'for ever' with a local florist for six red roses to adorn Marilyn's memorial.***

LOST CIVILIZATIONS

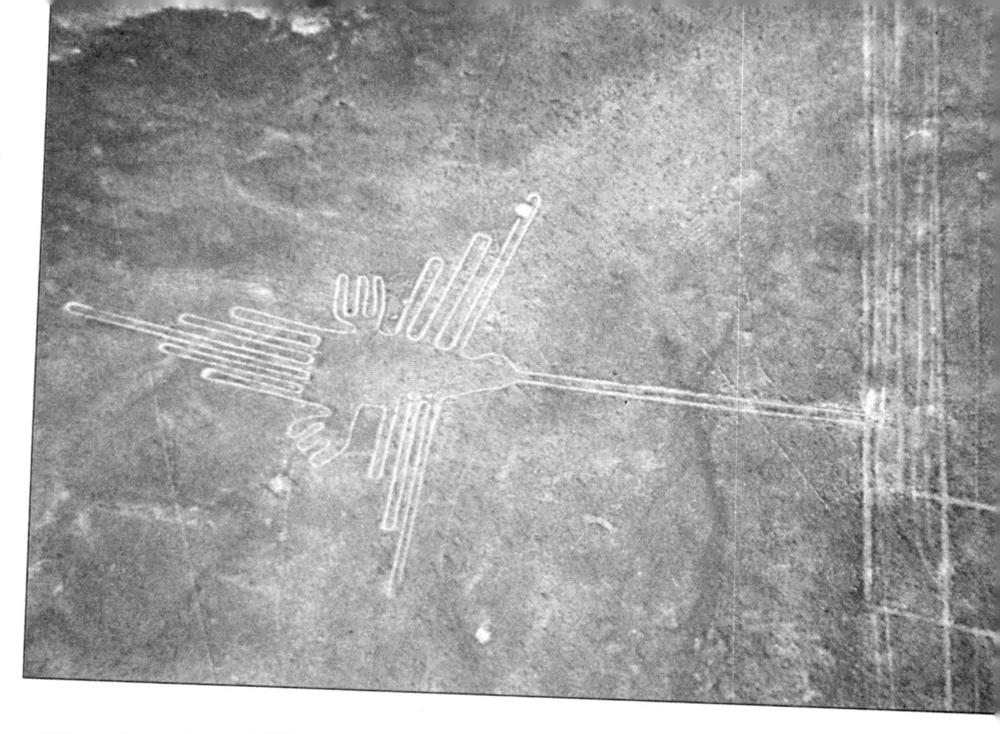

Wealth and wisdom beyond the wildest dreams – or mere fairy-tales? What is the truth about Atlantis, paradise lost; the fabulous El Dorado, a mythical city of gold; and, perhaps strangest of all, the extraordinary knowledge of the priests of an ancient tribe who still worship their guardians from a distant star?

It is the most fascinating exploration of all … the search for a city, a land, even a civilization the existence of which no one can be certain. By word of mouth over hundreds of years, stories have tantalized the inquisitive. Tales of fabled countries, of idyllic landscapes, of sophisticated cultures – sometimes of unimaginable wealth.

Were these lost civilizations the result of a sudden flowering of the human spirit? Were they the result of visitations from another world? Why did they arise … and why did they die?

Once upon a time the Sahara desert was green; rock paintings prove that a pastoral people dwelt there 5,000 years ago. A stone city stands testament to the lost civilization of Zimbabwe; centuries ago it was the heart of an African trading empire. Perfect geometrical patterns criss-cross the desolate plains of Peru; they were created by the Nazca Indians 1,500 years ago and could not be replicated even today.

Who were these peoples who came and went and left so little trace of their

Above: ***These marks in the desert suggest the Nazca Indians possessed some long-forgotten knowledge.***

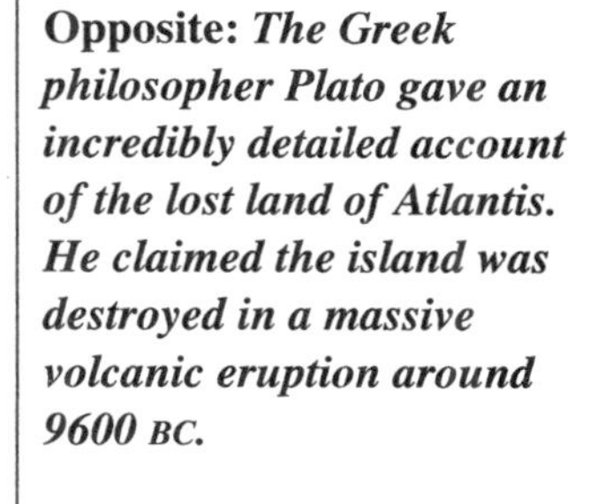

Opposite: ***The Greek philosopher Plato gave an incredibly detailed account of the lost land of Atlantis. He claimed the island was destroyed in a massive volcanic eruption around 9600 BC.***

Left: ***An artist's impression of the idyllic Atlantean lifestyle.***

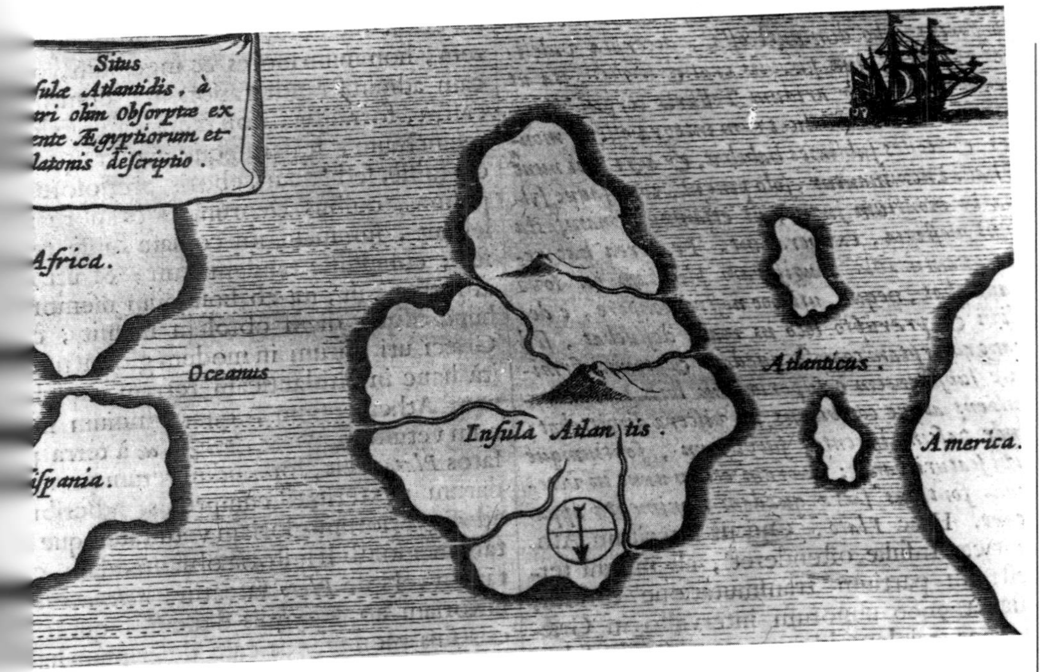

Above: ***This 1665 engraving showing the position of Atlantis is based on Plato's assertion that it lies 'beyond the pillars of Hercules' – the Straits of Gibraltar.***

Below: The Temple of Poseidon was said to be a shrine of breathtaking beauty.

existence so many centuries ago?

Here we examine three of the most enticing mysteries of all: at sea, on land and, strangest of all, in the skies …

AN EARTHLY PARADISE

Talk of a 'lost city' and the mystical name of Atlantis immediately springs to mind. According to legend, a people of great wealth, beauty and happiness inhabited this island paradise. Few great unanswer mysteries can have had as much ener thought and words expended upon them that surrounding Atlantis, supposed blessed with lush vegetation, a cultured a civilized populace, a wealth of natu minerals including gold and silver, a food in abundance.

Did this paradise on Earth exist? Wh was it? And what was the catastrophe t destroyed it?

The ancient Greek philosopher Pl was the source of legends about the gr kingdom and city of Atlantis, whi vanished from the face of the Ea centuries before the birth of Christ. 347 BC he wrote an account of how, a young man, he was listening to Socra and Critias discussing philosophy wit group of friends. They described kingdom 'derived from historical traditi – a once-great nation whose people beca corrupt and whose leaders led it i decline. According to the Egyptian prie quoted by Critias, it was destroyed a violent volcanic eruption, followed b tidal wave which plunged the tragic isla beneath the waves forever.

According to Plato, the date of destruction of Atlantis was around 9500 It was sited, he says, 'beyond the Pillars

Hercules' (or Straits of Gibraltar). He describes the magical land in incredible detail. He talks of its magnificent hot and cold springs, the elaborate temples, the luxurious accommodation afforded to visiting royalty. In all, he paints a splendid picture of a kingdom which enjoyed, before its decline and fall, the greatest benefits of civilization. He says:

'At the centre of the island, near the sea, was a plain, said to be the most beautiful and fertile of all plains, and near the middle of this plain ... a hill of no great size. In the centre was a shrine sacred to Poseidon and Cleito, surrounded by a golden wall through which entry was forbidden.'

Because of Plato's account, Atlantis has become a holy grail for many adventurers, archeologists, historians and others fascinated with legends. But not one of them has been able to find the submerged remains of the ancient utopia.

Theories on the real identity and location of Atlantis have been endless, and the search to substantiate them fruitless. One eminent American politician, Congressman Ignatius Donnelly, sparked the modern-day interest in the lost kingdom when, in 1882, he published two works on the subject – *Atlantis the Antediluvian World*, and *Ragnarok, the Age of Fire*. His account put Atlantis, a huge continent which thrived and prospered for centuries before sinking beneath the waves for ever, in the middle of the Atlantic Ocean, .

But sadly for Atlantis enthusiasts, most of his theories have been debunked. The vast ridge in the Atlantic which runs from Iceland to Tristan da Cunha is not sinking – in fact, it is rising, and has been doing so for thousands of years.

Another theorist claimed that the eels which migrated to the Sargasso Sea had a memory of a freshwater source which once existed there, and that the 2.5 million square miles of weed that float on the sea off Florida hide the site of a submerged city. Both theories, unfortunately, are false.

Eel migration is now regarded as being no more mysterious than the migratory habits of birds, and the weed does not shroud a dead city; it is merely a perfectly natural phenomenon, carried by swirling currents off the Florida coastline.

Others have earmarked the Scilly Isles off Cornwall's coast as a possibility, and have raised the theory of a great land-bridge between Britain and America via Iceland and Greenland, or have speculated that the mysterious sunken island was even in the Pacific Ocean. All these theories have been scotched by the experts over the years.

An American photographer, Edgar Cayce, claimed to have seen into the past and mentally visited Atlantis between 1923 and his death in 1945. He said he had never read Plato but described the island in the way the Greek philosopher did. He said Atlantis had been destroyed by a great nuclear explosion when its gifted citizenry had learned how to split the atom. He further prophesied that 'a portion of the temples' would be discovered in 1969.

In that very year, archeologist Dr J. Manson Valentine was taken by a local fisherman known as Bonefish Sam to view curious rectangular stones lying in eight metres of water north of Paradise Point on the tiny Bahamian island of Bimini.

Valentine was ecstatic. He believed the two parallel lines of stones, about half a mile long and five yards square, to be the remnants of a great harbour wall. Divers and archeologists arrived in hordes, probing to see whether the stones were the work of Aztec, Toltec, Mayan, or any one of a number of other civilizations.

No one has yet been able to prove or

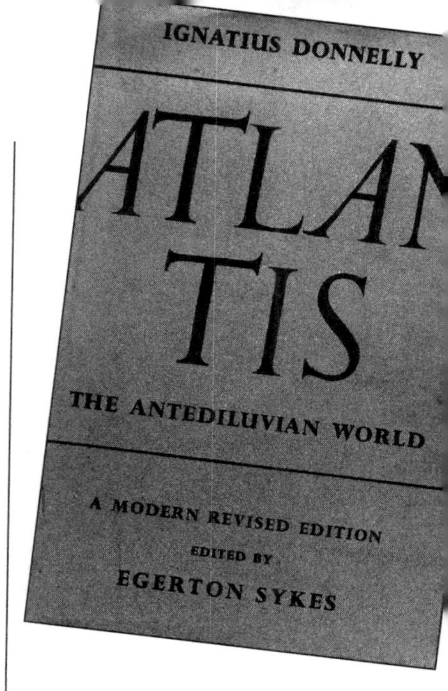

Above: ***Congressman Donnelly's book started the modern-day Atlantis cult.***

THE PHOTOGRAPHER CLAIMED HE HAD 'VISITED' ATLANTIS AND PROPHESIED THAT THE ANCIENT CITY WOULD BE FOUND.

Below: ***How Atlantis fitted onto the early maps.***

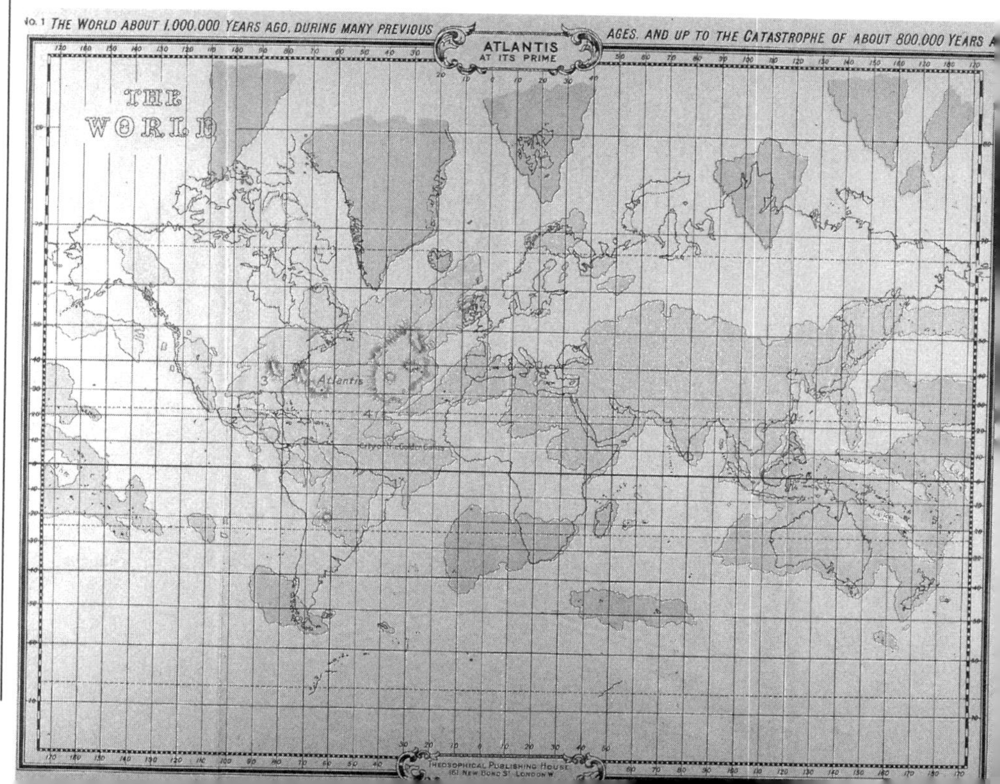

Above: ***The cover of* Fate *magazine reports another false dawn for believers in the lost city.***

Above right: ***Further interpretation of Plato's detailed description of Atlantis – a banqueting hall.***

Below: ***The ruins of a Minoan town in the aftermath of the eruption.***

disprove that the stones were man-made, or whether they were indeed part of the ancient lost city of Atlantis. One eminent professor, Dr John Hall of Miami University, declared in 1970 that the wall was in fact a natural phenomenon called pleistocene beachrock, adding: 'Therefore, alas, for those who believe in the old legend, another Atlantis is dismissed'. However, two later expeditions to Bimini in 1975 and 1977 revealed a block of stone with a carved edge, something definitely crafted by a human hand. Its origins still remain a mystery.

A FIERY FURNACE

Many academics subscribe to the notion that, since the Atlantis described by Plato has never been found, the philosopher must have mistaken the location. The catastrophe he refers to, they believe, was in fact the mighty volcanic eruption which blasted the Minoan civilization off the face of the Earth.

Derek Ager, head of the Department of Geology at Bristol University, believes that this may be what happened: 'I have no doubt at all that there never was such a land mass beyond the Pillars of Hercules. The subject is just not worth discussing. On the other hand, I think it is quite possible, even probable, that the legend refers to the destruction of the Minoan civilization by the volcanic process.'

The centre of Minoan culture was the city of Knossos, on the island of Crete. From here the Minoans dominated the Aegean and the islands clustered in it. In 1967, the Greek archeologist Spyridon Marinatos began excavating on one of those islands, Kalliste. There he discovered the remains of a city which was to become known as the 'Pompeii of the Aegean' because, like its famous Roman companion in fate, it was destroyed by volcanic eruptions of such magnitude as to defy belief.

Kalliste, as the island was called in ancient times, is now termed Santorini or Thera, and is the southernmost of the Cyclades islands. There, buried beneath 100 feet of volcanic ash, Marinatos discovered the first sign of the tragedy which wiped out the inhabitants.

Scientists now believe that a volcanic

eruption four times greater than that which destroyed the Indonesian isle of Krakatoa in 1883 was responsible for the destruction of Kalliste. To give some idea of the scale of such an explosion, Krakatoa, when it erupted, produced the loudest bang in recorded history, spewing rocks, lava, ash and fire over a huge area. The volcanic ash cloud was carried as far away as Europe and the resulting tidal waves crossed the Pacific Ocean and damaged boats on the coast of South America. And this was only a quarter of the force of the explosion which ripped the ancient civilization on Kalliste asunder.

It is believed that when the Minoans were warned of their impending fate by minor earthquakes and eruptions, they took to the sea in boats and were probably no more than 70 miles away when the main eruptions occurred, raining down burning debris and choking ash upon their vessels. Whichever ships escaped the firestorm would have been smashed to matchsticks by the resultant tidal waves.

Some historians even suggest that the ash clouds could be the origin of the story of the Egyptian plagues described in the Old Testament, since they covered an area greater than 15,500 square miles and would easily have been visible as far away as Egypt.

So was the Atlantis described by Plato the Bronze Age Minoan culture which blossomed in the islands of the Aegean? We may never know. The golden age of Minoan civilization was utterly destroyed. All the human remains that have been found were blackened by ash or badly charred by fire, but it is known that the Minoans were a cultured people, civilized and refined; they enjoyed mains drainage and baths in their homes, unrivalled prosperity and command of the seas.

For 500 years the Minoans ruled supreme ... and then vanished. The mysterious island of Santorini or Kalliste is the most likely candidate for the site of ancient Atlantis. Plato's oft-retold story was probably no fairy-tale after all.

THE ANCIENT CIVILIZATION WAS BLOWN OFF THE FACE OF THE EARTH IN A SPECTACULAR EXPLOSION.

Above: ***This Minoan mosaic is typical of an art form which is still revered the world over.***

Left: ***A Minoan snake goddess. Idols such as this were worshipped by the proud and wealthy islanders.***

THE GOLDEN CITY OF EL DORADO

In many ways, the search for the lost city of El Dorado is even more tantalizing than that for Atlantis. The principal reason is the fabled wealth that lay within its walls. But the other reason is that whereas Atlantis was engulfed by the seas, El Dorado still exists in some form – and its golden age is much more recent.

The story of El Dorado begins with the Inca empire of Peru. When the Spaniards invaded the Incas in 1530, they discovered a civilized race, beautiful public buildings, an ordered society – and hoards of gold.

Capturing the city of Cuzco, the Spanish Conquistadors discovered plunder beyond their avaricious dreams. Golden art

Above: A *Conquistador* landing party. These greedy men were totally ruthless in their pursuit of gold.

treasures abounded: there was gold-plating on the temple walls and even the palace water pipes were made of gold.

But it was not enough for the invaders. The Spaniards captured the Inca emperor Atahuallpa and held him to ransom, demanding that a room 22 feet by 17 feet be filled to the ceiling with gold. The innocent Incas set about collecting this extraordinary ransom. With the room full of the precious metal, they waited patiently for the release of their emperor.

The ruthless conquerors, led by the illiterate but militarily brilliant Francisco Pizarro, reneged on the deal and cold-bloodedly killed their hostage. Then they embarked on a terrible reign of looting and pillaging, stripping the entire Inca empire of its age-old wealth. Still not content with their booty, the Spaniards began to look further afield for even greater treasure chests.

That is when they first heard the name El Dorado.

Myth and legend and fact all merge when El Dorado is mentioned. It was thus even in Pizarro's time. The conquerors were told that El Dorado was a mountain of solid gold lying to the north of Inca territory, so they marched to a treasure-filled temple hidden deep in the jungle.

Expeditions were sent into the jungle. The sole survivor of one of them, Juan Martin de Albujar, returned with stories of being held within a secret Inca capital and being freed with as much gold as he and his men could carry. All had been lost in the jungle, he said.

Another conquistador, Sebastian de Belalcazar who founded the Ecuador capital of Quito, heard the stories and coined the name El Dorado. But he failed to find it.

It was not only the Spanish who attempted to reach El Dorado. Between 1535 and 1540 several expeditions led by different colonial powers sought the 'lost city'. Georg Hohermuth, the German governor of Venezuela, followed the Indian salt trade routes, having learned from the natives that 'where the salt comes from, comes gold'. He set out with 400 men, searched for three years, encountered starvation and pestilence, and passed within 60 miles of the site of El Dorado. He returned empty handed, leaving 300 of his expedition dead in the jungle. Another German adventurer, Nicholaus Federmann, embarked on the same mission with as little success.

A hard-headed Spanish lawyer, Gonzalo Jimenez de Quesada, led the largest expedition to find the legendary golden hoard. In 1536 he headed inland from the Colombian coast with 900 men. Each step of the way had to be carved out with machetes. Disease and battles with the Chibcha Indians reduced their numbers to 200.

Quesada captured villages and tortured the inhabitants until they revealed the source of their precious metals and gems. He thought he had stumbled upon El Dorado when an Indian led him to the town of Hunsa, described as the 'place of gold'. Quesada looted gold plates and

large hoards of emeralds and bags of gold dust. The chief's house, lined with massive sheets of gold and containing a beautiful throne of gold and emeralds, was similarly sacked. The Spaniards slaughtered all before them, even stealing the gold rings from the ears and noses of the dead Indians.

THE LAKE OF GOLD

At last Quesada's expedition came to a lake 9,000 feet above sea level. And it was here that the legend of El Dorado had been born …

El Dorado, as the natives told them, was not a place but a person. El Dorado is Spanish for 'The Gilded One', probably the chief of the Muisca nation who lived in the

THE GREEDY SPANIARDS SLAUGHTERED THE BEWILDERED INDIANS AND RIPPED THE GOLD RINGS FROM THEIR EARS AND NOSES.

Left: ***Pizarro. He kidnapped an Inca emperor and demanded a room 22 feet by 17 feet be filled with gold to pay the ransom.***

Below: ***Conquistadors setting dogs on Aztecs. A more evil, heartless bunch of men would be hard to find.***

region which now surrounds the Colombian capital of Bogota.

The chief of the Muiscas was crowned in a unique ritual. His tribe would gather in a holy valley in the mountains for several days of prayer and celebrations. The climax of the festival was a boat trip onto Lake Guatavita. Incense was burned and flutes wafted their music across the waters until the boat reached the centre of the perfectly circular lake.

The new chief was then stripped naked while priests coated his entire body with gold dust. It must have been a hugely religious experience for the watching crowds as, with the sun glinting on his body, the king made his offerings to the gods by lifting up gold treasures and dropping them into the deep waters of Lake Guatavita. He would then bathe in the lake to wash off the gold dust covering his body. Apparently, this was a signal for the onlookers to take their golden tributes and throw them from the shore into the lake.

Right: ***This gold disk with dancing figure was a primitive artform much sought after by the Conquistadors.***

Below: ***One of the golden treasures which central American Indian tribes would offer up to their gods.***

Lake Guatavita thereby held th riche hoard of gold that even the Conquis adors Spain could imagine. But they nev r fou El Dorado – the man or the place or he gol

In their ignorance, the poor Ind ans h neglected to tell their greedy torme ntors two vital facts. One was that El Do rado longer existed; the last Muisca chi ef to enthroned on the lake had been de posed few years earlier.

The second vital fact was hat Dorado's people had no source of gold their own; they gathered it by combination of war and trading salt

With the realization that the only way find any of El Dorado's gold was t plun the depths of Lake Guatavita, Qu esada brother Herman journeyed back to the si in 1545. He conscripted slave labo among the poor Muisca Indians an plac them in a human chain from the water edge to the top of the mou ntain Laboriously, they took water from he la in buckets and passed it along the li e to tipped away. After three mo ths continuous toil, the level of the l ke wa lowered by 9 feet. Herman Q uesad eventually abandoned the task, bu he d recover several hundred gold artefa ts fro the receding waters.

Several more ambitious sc heme followed. In 1585, another Spaniar whos name is now lost to history recruite 8,00 Indians to cut a deep channel to d ain th lake. This time the level fell by 60 eet an many more golden objects were un overe before landslips blocked the dr ainag channel.

A British company tried to dr in th lake at the beginning of this cen ury b drilling a tunnel which lowered the water level, but the mud on the lake bed was at first too soft and deep to walk on – and once the sun had baked it, was too hard to dig through. Ludicrously, by the time fresh equipment could be transported to the site, mud had blocked the drainage channels and rains had filled the lake again!

Happily for the region, the Colombian government passed legislation protecting the site from treasure-hunters, but the fabled wealth of El Dorado still haunts explorers, adventurers and treasure seekers. For not all the gold ended up in the bottom of Lake Guatavita. There is no shortage of those who would still kill for the greedy dream of Andean gold. The mystery of El Dorado lives on …

Above: *A colourful portrayal of the Spanish treasure seekers. The llama needed to be strong. Apart from its rider, it was expected to carry bulky and heavy items of plunder.*

SECRETS OF THE UNIVERSE

If the people of Atlantis had a civilization beyond belief, and the people of El Dorado had wealth beyond the dreams of avarice, what of the poor people of the Dogon tribe of Africa? They survive today, owning virtually nothing. Yet for centuries they have possessed the most astonishing scientific knowledge.

The Dogon tribe of West Africa live in a scattering of villages over a vast area of what is now the Republic of Mali. The terrain is rocky and arid, and their homes are built of mud and straw. Their life-style is primitive in the extreme by any Western standards. Yet extraordinarily, these primitive folk had detailed knowledge about stars and planets many hundreds of years before they were observed scientifically.

Have they and other primitive peoples gained their knowledge from other, greater, earlier civilizations? Or even from visitors from other planets?

The fascination with the Dogons comes because of a relatively recent scientific discovery. The glittering star Sirius, one of the brightest in the heavens, has a companion star which is so outshone by its near-neighbour that its very existence was not even suspected by astronomers until the 19th century. Invisible to the naked eye, this smaller star's nature was not revealed until the 1920s.

Yet the existence of Sirius B was known about hundreds, if not thousands, of years ago. It was recorded by a people whose primitive existence offers no outward clue to the extraordinary astronomical knowledge they have.

When French anthropologists Marcel Griaule and Germaine Dieterlen studied the Dogons, living amongst them and winning their confidence, they discovered a depth of knowledge of the Universe that astounded them. They found that when this race migrated to West Africa and settled on the Bandiagra Plateau some time between the 13th and 16th centuries, they brought with them secrets that they could not be expected to know today.

Not too surprisingly, they knew that the Earth was round and spun on its own north–south axis; they knew that the Earth and the other planets revolved around the Sun; they knew that our Moon was 'dry

HOW COULD THE PRIMITIVE NATIVES HAVE KNOWN ABOUT THE GLITTERING STAR THOUSANDS OF YEARS AGO WHEN ASTRONOMERS DENIED ITS VERY EXISTENCE UNTIL RECENTLY?

and dead like dry dead blood'. For some reason, they knew that the Milky Way was shaped like a spiral – a fact impossible to detect without extremely expensive astronomical equipment.

Without access to powerful telescopes, they could not have been expected to know that Saturn was surrounded by its famous rings – yet they drew the planet with its halo in the dirt outside their huts. Even more incredible was that they knew that Jupiter had four main moons – impossible knowledge for any but the most sophisticated race.

Amazing as they were, the revelations about Jupiter's moons and other aspects of the Solar System paled into insignificance when compared with what the Dogons knew about more distant bodies.

Right: ***An engraving of the ornamental representation of the Dog-star.***

Below: ***A Dogon village in Mali. Primitive … yet these people had an incredible depth of knowledge of the Universe.***

Lying at the heart of their beliefs about the Universe is the star Sirius, to them the brightest in the galaxy. The Dogons studied and charted all the various stars and planets that passed around and interacted with Sirius in the night sky – in particular, the path of Sirius B.

As author Francis Hitching reported in his *World Atlas of Mysteries*, Sirius B is 100,000 times less bright than Sirius itself. 'Yet,' said Hitching, 'the Dogon not only knew about this star but many of its characteristics.' He said they knew that it was white and although it was 'the smallest thing there is' it was also 'the heaviest star' made of a substance 'heavier than all the iron on Earth'. Hitching said this was a good description of Sirius B's density, which is so great that a single cubic metre weighs 20,000 tons.

Dogon drawings revealed the true orbit of Sirius B around Sirius – an elliptical path that accurately positioned the two stars over a timespan of 50 years, the

Above: ***Wall coverings Dogon style. These decorations were used to adorn the walls of meeting houses. They often told the life story of one or more elders.***

Above: ***These Dogon granaries are evidence of a remarkably advanced civilization.***

HE HOPED THE TRIBE'S HISTORY WOULD PROVIDE A VITAL CLUE TO ITS FANTASTIC KNOWLEDGE.

Opposite: ***This Dogon dancer in his mud mask would have been a common sight at festival times.***

correct period for a complete orbit. As Griaule and Dieterlen wrote: 'The problem of knowing how, with no instruments at their disposal, men could know of the movements and certain characteristics of virtually invisible stars has not been settled.'

CREATURES FROM ANOTHER WORLD

In 1946 Marcel Griaule was allowed by the Dogon priests to share their innermost secrets. Any discoveries he had by then made counted almost as nought compared with what he now heard. For the Dogons told him that they had learned their extensive knowledge from visitors to Earth who came from a planet orbiting Sirius B.

The French anthropologist was astounded. And when he published his learned papers he was met with predictable scepticism. But there could be no doubt that Marcel Griaule had told the truth. He lived among the Dogons for 21 years and when he died in 1956 about 250,000 people attended his funeral in Mali.

His research was immediately taken up by other fascinated scientists and authors. American scholar Robert Temple set to work to trace more clearly the Dogons' movements before their arrival at the Bandiagara Plateau. Temple believed that the tribe's history might provide the vital clue to its fantastic knowledge.

The two million members of the Dogon and associated tribes arrived in an area about 250 miles south of Timbuktu between 400 and 700 years ago. They had migrated there from the north-east, probably having originated in North Africa, in what is now Libya. The tribe's closest neighbours at the time would have been Egyptian, but Temple found no key to the Dogon beliefs from that source. However, the mythology of ancient Greece and of Babylon did provide some clues.

In both Greek and Babylonian legend there are stories of creatures from another world who had supernatural powers and who passed on astronomical and astrological knowledge to the inhabitants of Earth. In both cases, these alien creatures were amphibian and they helped civilize this planet.

In his book, *The Sirius Mystery*, Robert Temple claims that the Dogons worshipped extra-terrestrial visitors who landed in the Persian Gulf in far distant times. The tribe called these creatures Nommos and have worshipped them ever since. Dogon drawings show a whirling, descending spacecraft or ark, peopled by the Nommos who are described as 'the monitor of the universe, the father of mankind, guardian of its spiritual principles, dispenser of rain and master of water'.

What further evidence supports the Dogon claims of a previous civilization brought to them by the heavens? Is it not all fantasy and mumbo-jumbo?

When Marcel Griaule first wrote his reports detailing the strange knowledge of the Dogons, they included one piece of information that seemed to make no sense whatsoever. The Dogons claimed that there was a *third* star in orbit around Sirius – a 'Sirius C'. This third star also influenced Sirius's movement in the heavens, despite the fact that it was four times lighter in weight than Sirius B.

At the time of the French reports, there was no evidence for a third star. The idea of a 'Sirius C' weakened rather than strengthened the case. But now, many years later, astronomers have detected such a star - possibly what they call a 'red dwarf'. Just as the Dogons have always believed. Just as they recorded when the Western world was young but their civilization was already old, many centuries ago.

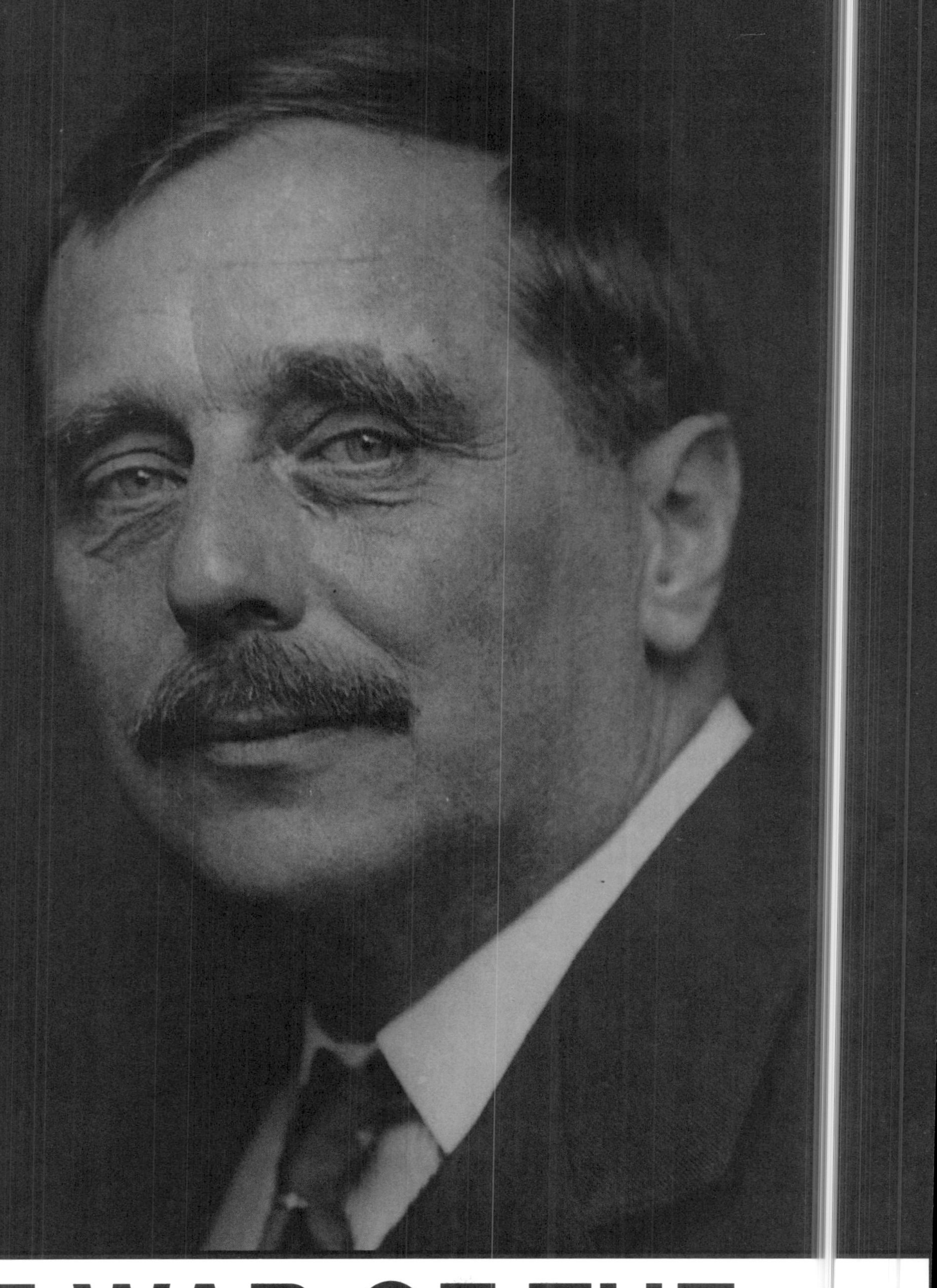

THE WAR OF THE WORLDS

It started as an ordinary radio broadcast, but mounting panic and hysteria spread across America as the frightened voices of the announcers told their terrified listeners that the unbelievable had happened. Martians had invaded the Earth.

'Ladies and gentlemen, I have a grave announcement to make.'

That was the sentence that instantly concentrated the minds of millions of Americans as they tuned in to their radios on the night of Sunday, 30 October 1938. It also heralded the start of one of the most effective, and embarrassing, hoaxes the world has ever seen.

That night thousands upon thousands of people in the most powerful nation on Earth would flee their homes convinced that America had been invaded by men from Mars.

They paid the price for keeping only half an ear on the radio. For at 8 pm the CBS continuity announcer had faithfully informed his audience: 'The Columbia Broadcasting System and affiliated stations present Orson Welles and his Mercury Theatre of the Air in *The War of the Worlds* by H.G. Wells.'

Then came Welles's thunderous voice: 'We now know that in the early years of the 20th century, this world was being watched closely by intelligences greater than man's.' Clear enough surely: a live radio play with a script pretty close to the work of the original author. But at 24 Welles was already a master of building atmosphere, lulling an audience in readiness to shock them.

Before his opening lines were complete another actor took the microphone to interrupt with what sounded like a routine weather bulletin: 'Tonight's weather ... For

Opposite: *Master of sci-fi H.G. Wells. His novel* **The War of the Worlds** *was transformed by Orson Welles into a gripping – and believable – piece of radio drama.*

Below: *A poster advertising the film of the book. Thousands queued to watch it.*

the next 24 hours there will be not much change in temperature. A slight atmospheric disturbance of undetermined origin is reported over Nova Scotia, causing a low pressure area to move down rather rapidly over the north-eastern states, bringing a forecast of rain, accompanied by winds of light-gale force.

'Maximum temperature 66, minimum 48. This weather report comes to you from the Government Weather Bureau.

'We now take you to the Meridian Room at the Hotel Park Plaza in downtown New York where you will be entertained by the music of Ramon Raquello and his orchestra.'

So already many of the families who had tuned in from the start of the performance were receiving confused signals. Was this in fact a play? Perhaps not. Perhaps the Mercury Theatre was on another night. Or maybe father had got the time wrong. Either way the Raquello Orchestra sounded decent enough listening for the time being.

Welles had another, unforeseen advantage up his sleeve. He had come up with *The War of the Worlds* 'real life' scenario as a way to boost his show's pitiful ratings, grab a chunk of good publicity (if it worked) and persuade a sponsor to come in to offer a little security. Most important of all was to lure a few listeners from a rival station's popular Charlie McCarthy show, which went out at the same time.

The stakes were high. This was a last-ditch bid by Welles really to launch his Mercury Theatre. He'd been told on the quiet that unless there was some sign of an

Below: ***The staff of Grover's Mill, New Jersey, talk over Welles's hoax the day after the 'war'. According to the radio play, the first aliens landed at the mill.***

Above: ***A scene from Paramount's 1953 version of*** **The War of the Worlds** ***shows Martian spaceships hunting Earthmen.***

improvement in the ratings the whole show was doomed.

AN INVASION FROM OUTER SPACE

That night, as it happened, Charlie McCarthy wasn't exactly hooking more fans. He had a new, totally unknown, crooner on and by around 10 past 8 people were getting bored. A few switched off but the majority began fiddling with their sets to see if there was anything a bit more interesting on CBS. They would not be disappointed.

Amid the crackles and high-pitched whines they suddenly realized that some kind of major news story was breaking along the country's east coast. CBS seemed to have a scoop – a scoop that was unfolding as they listened. Excitedly, families across the nation huddled around their radios to listen. None of the McCarthy defectors could have had the faintest clue that they were hearing a piece of drama.

'Ladies and gentlemen,' went the level voice, 'I have a grave announcement to make. The strange object which fell at Grover's Mill, New Jersey, earlier this evening was not a meteorite. Incredible as it seems it contained strange beings who are believed to be the vanguard of an army from the planet Mars.'

Then gentle, calming music – a masterpiece in terms of effect, for it gave the impression that the government had taken control of the media and was attempting to allay fears by playing familiar musical scores. Of course, the reaction was just the opposite – 'What's happening? Why won't someone tell us what's going on? Where's the president? Who's fighting who?'

This continued for several minutes, building up the stress levels of the audience almost to breaking point. Then the announcer again. This time the smooth statement had gone to be replaced by a whiff of panic. The voice had an edge to it as it told how the leathery-skinned Martians had started spreading out along New Jersey. Police were mobilizing to try and hold them back.

Then came more hurried announcements

and ominous silences. By now listeners were calling in neighbours and phoning relatives in other states. It had taken only a few minutes to infect a large chunk of America with alien-fever.

When word finally came of terrifying battles along the eastern seaboard it was the last straw. Thousands did what came naturally. They jumped in their cars and headed for the hills.

Below: ***Welles gets into his part. This picture was taken during the broadcast.***

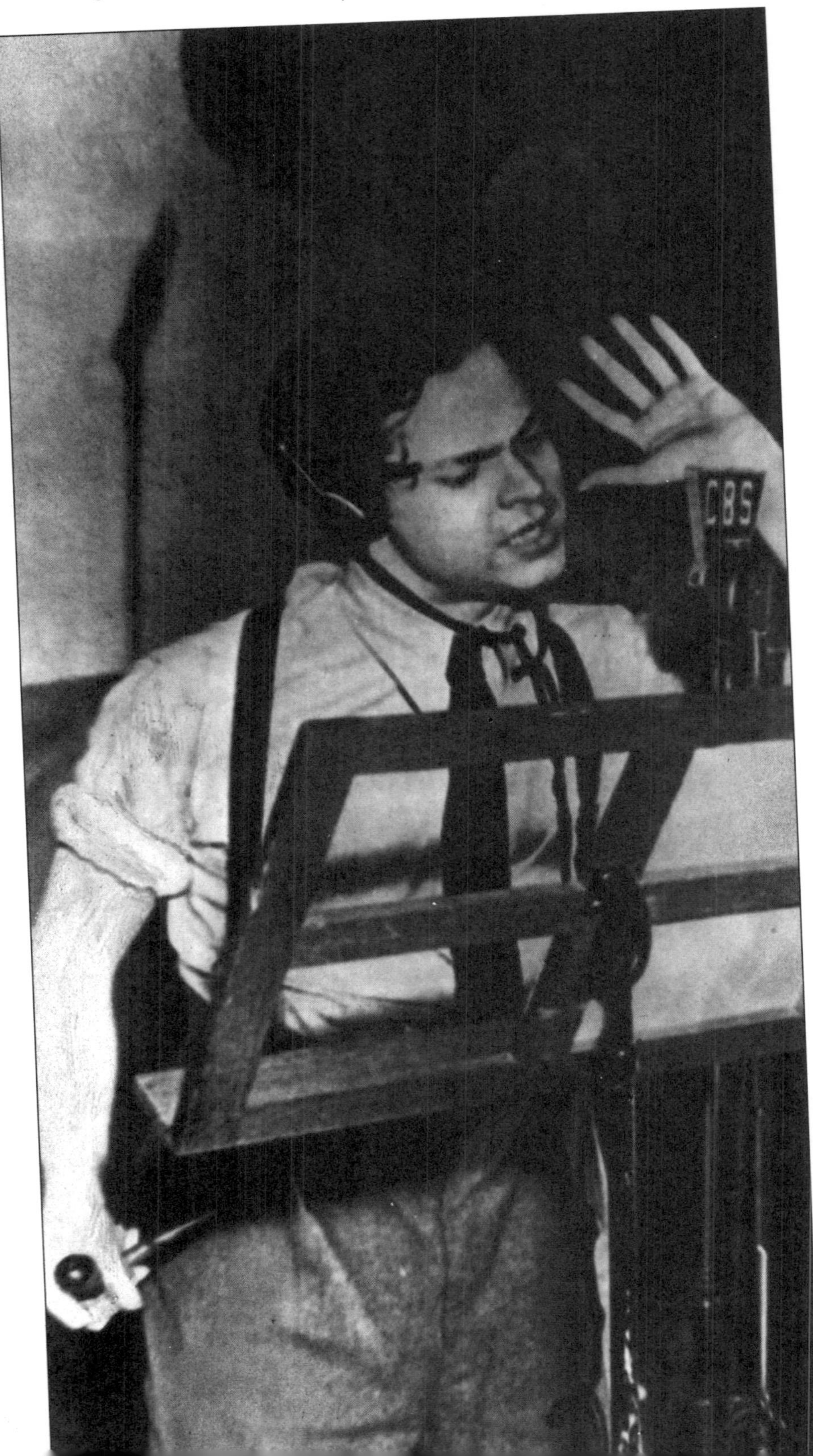

This, it must be said, was not exactly how Welles had planned it. Sure, he wanted to shock. Yes, he hoped this particular play would be a totally original piece of radio drama. And if a story found its way into the papers, well, who knew what spin-offs there might be from prospective sponsors.

Welles and his team – Paul Stewart and John Houseman – had been sweating blood on this particular play for several days. It was to be the 17th in the current Mercury Theatre series but never before had they experienced such creative tension.

Resetting the play in America (the original work centred the action in London) was not so difficult. Neither was adapting it for what could easily be a family audience, though the scenes in which Martians drank the blood of their human victims were skimmed over.

No, Welles argued, it needed more shock value, more realism. It needed to sound a less than perfect production if it was to be a success.

On the Thursday before broadcast the three men gathered to hear the results of their labours to date. They heard a tape – the final product of countless script revisions and several rehearsals. They were not pleased with their achievement.

Welles, the lynchpin of the whole operation, was by now almost on his knees. He'd been rehearsing for another play in New York by day, switching to the Mercury team at night. Production assistants would recall later how he looked as depressed as anyone had ever seen him. He seemed like a poker player locked into a game where the stakes were increasing too fast. His pep talk to the team suggested he was ready to gamble his already considerable reputation on a one-off which might, or might not, work.

'Our only chance is to make it as realistic as possible,' he said. 'We'll have to throw in as many stunts as we can think of.'

BLOODCURDLING SCREAM

The production team burnt the midnight oil, adding real-life sound bites and clips from news reels onto the backing tapes. The next day Stewart perfected the sound of a panicking crowd, screams and gunfire

– the vital additions that would later fool the nation.

As the minutes ticked down to broadcast time the studio itself looked like it had hosted an inter-galactic war. Overflowing ashtrays, half-empty coffee cups and half-eaten sandwiches all bore tribute to the brainstorming sessions of the last 72 hours. But as Welles stepped towards the microphone, downing a cold bottle of pineapple juice in the process, the general feeling was of excitement – of producing a show which genuinely could break new ground.

The *coup de grâce* was delivered towards the end, at a time when the exodus of a terrified population was already well underway. The announcer crackled back onto air to reveal: 'We take you now to Washington for a special broadcast on the national emergency by the Secretary of the Interior.'

Welles got an actor to impersonate the politician in question. The official line was to urge people not to panic, though to make it clear that the Martian assault was now well underway. Not only New Jersey but the whole of the country was now experiencing the sight of spacecrafts landing by the dozen. Thousands of police, state troopers and civilians had already

Above: ***Ain't takin' no chances. This veteran needed some persuading to put down his shotgun after Welles's broadcast.***

AS THE NEWS CAME OF FEROCIOUS BATTLES ALONG THE EASTERN SEABOARD, THOUSANDS OF PEOPLE FLED FOR THE HILLS.

WHOLE FAMILIES BELIEVED THAT BRIGHTLY COLOURED WET TOWELS WRAPPED AROUND THEIR HEADS WOULD PROTECT THEM FROM THE NERVE GAS.

died horrible deaths under the wilting fire of ray guns.

There were the inevitable eyewitness accounts, many of them arriving courtesy of the superb actor Joseph Cotton. Of how fireballs which turned out to be spacecraft landed from nowhere. Of how terrifying beings emerged from them and started the killing. Then a step further. A voice sounding suspiciously like the president's came on warning people of the dangers of panic. The show ended with the strangled tones of the announcer shouting from the top of the CBS building that Manhattan was being occupied by a ruthless and hideous army. His last line was a blood-curdling scream, though by now most of the listeners were too busy trying to escape to take it in.

MASS PANIC

In New Jersey, site of the first landings, the roads were clogged solid with automobiles heading for the countryside. Whole families were seen emerging from their homes with brightly coloured wet towels wrapped around their heads – a recommended way of surviving the nerve gases they had been warned about. Valuables and prized possessions were being loaded into pickups and lorries ready for the trip out to the sticks. Evacuation had begun.

In New York City desperate wives tried in vain to call constantly engaged bars in search of their husbands. Crowds poured from restaurants and theatres as word spread like wildfire. Bus terminals and taxi ranks choked under the pressure of demand.

Even the US Navy was successfully conned. Sailors were ordered back to their ships in readiness to make a last stand against the invaders. Reports of meteor showers emerged from across the land. Some imaginative souls even tried to pretend they had had a close encounter with one of the aliens.

Troopers phoned their admin HQs to volunteer to defend America. Congregations spilled out of church services, some of the faithful predicting that this was, in fact, what had been promised all along – the coming of the Lord. In the South terrified women fell to their knees and prayed and according to later news reports there was even one attempted suicide.

Newspapers and radio stations fielded literally thousands of calls between them. Yet no one apparently stopped to wonder why all was sweetness and light over at CBS, where Welles was just bringing the show to a climax with threats of immediate martial law. He hadn't a clue what was going on outside.

The station did receive a lot of calls, which were all passed on to Welles and Cotton. Cotton dismissed them out of hand as 'just cranks' and although two policemen turned up at CBS with orders to find out what was happening those officers didn't mention the dramas being unveiled outside. Instead they just hung around, realizing the broadcast was make-believe, and enjoyed the final stages.

The first Welles found out about the effects of his legendary show came the following morning when he couldn't help but notice the wording on a huge advertising hoarding above the New York Times building.

It read: 'Orson Welles Causes Panic'.

He bought every paper he could find and revelled in headlines such as 'Attack from Mars in Radio Play Puts Thousands in Fear' or 'Radio Listeners in Panic – Many Flee Homes to Escape Gas Raids from Mars'.

Then came the backlash. A lot of egos had been bruised, macho icons demolished. Newspapers condemned the actor for being irresponsible and there followed a clutch of negligence writs against CBS amounting to a hefty $1.1 million. But later all the actions fizzled out and Orson Welles resumed his position as America's most lovable star.

CBS, meanwhile, congratulated itself for pulling off a superb and original stunt. The Mercury Theatre looked to be on the up and up and a long-awaited sponsor had at last come forward.

Radio's most influential show at last had a future.

In Britain there was a scathing response to the panic Welles had managed to induce. 'Only the Americans could get so worked up by a radio show,' was the typical reaction of the stiff-upper-lip brigade.

HOAXED!

Yet a sizeable section of Britain's TV viewing population is regularly hoaxed. One of the most convincing – too convincing, many argued later – was a TV drama called *Ghostwatch* which was broadcast on Halloween 1992. By the end of it the switchboards at BBC TV centre were jammed by thousands of worried callers and within hours one young man had killed himself in the apparent belief that he was about to become a victim of similar supernatural manifestations.

The *Ghostwatch* case is all the more remarkable because it had been clearly advertised in newspapers and trailed on TV as a drama, part of the BBC's Screen One series. But borrowing from the Welles school of spoofing, the producers quickly managed to persuade many people that what they were actually seeing was a serious, live TV investigation into spooky goings-on at a real haunted house.

The house in question was a totally fictitious council property in Northolt, Middlesex. The family who lived there, the Earlys, had apparently been plagued for years by a poltergeist whose specialities were lobbing plates and pouring out puddles into the middle of the carpet. This proved no problem for the BBC's special effects department.

There was also a belief that the two young Early sisters (the family roles were all played by actors) were exhibiting symptoms of possession.

In the same way Welles had used a weather report and big band recital to convince his audience that they were no longer listening to a drama, the BBC producers had to find a way of blurring the line between fact and fantasy. To do that

THE SWITCHBOARD WAS JAMMED AND ONE POOR BOY HANGED HIMSELF IN TERROR.

Below: ***The aftermath. Orson Welles is 'doorstepped' by journalists eager for his version of events. His response: 'I had no idea the play would create such a furore.'***

Above: ***Martin Denham, who killed himself. His girlfriend said: 'The programme affected him badly.'***

HER HUSBAND WATCHED, POWERLESS AND HORRIFIED, AS SHE VANISHED INTO THIN AIR.

they employed three well-known presenters who each had some background in 'serious' television – Michael Parkinson, Mike Smith and Sarah Greene (Smith's real-life wife).

Parkinson played the anchorman of the team, switching between the studio and Northolt. Greene was the roving reporter out with the Earlys as they prepared for the night's hauntings. And Smith manned the phone lines to gauge reaction from viewers and monitor any other ghostly manifestations taking place around the country.

It looked for all the world like a live Halloween night special designed to fill a blank 90 minutes. Many among the millions of watchers must have been keeping only half an eye on the box, confidently expecting nothing would happen. They were wrong.

FIENDISH GHOUL

The plate smashing and puddle pouring was only the half of it. Clanking pipes, flying objects and flashing lights rammed home the impression that the BBC was filming a historic clip unique in the annals of broadcasting. Throughout it all analysis was provided by real-life experts in the paranormal – Maurice Gross, an authority on poltergeists, and Guy Lyon Playfair, author of a true account of the haunting of a house in Enfield, north London.

By the end many thousands were convinced that ghosts were, after all, real. And when Sarah Greene apparently vanished into thin air, the victim of some fiendish ghoul, the look of horror on her studio-bound husband's face set the first phones ringing on the BBC exchanges.

Perhaps the more impressionable viewers had read an interview with Sarah Greene in the newspapers earlier that week. In it she admitted she had already had a psychic experience on air and was rather nervous that the same thing could happen again.

She told one reporter: 'About ten years ago when making a documentary at the Royal Hospital in Chelsea I interviewed an old soldier who told me that the hospital had a regular ghostly visitor. He thought it was one of the original pensioners who seemed to hang around just to keep his eye on the old place.

'After the programme was transmitted I had dozens of calls from viewers who were sure that, while the old man was telling his story to me, they could see the ghost of the Chelsea Pensioner lingering near the staircase behind where we were sitting.

'We hadn't seen anything while we were filming, and we could see nothing out of the ordinary on the television monitor screen when we played back the interview.'

It was all good knockabout stuff. Interviewed afterwards, Michael Parkinson made a direct comparison with Welles's *The War of the Worlds* and observed: 'You always get some viewers believing all they see on television is real. If it does for my career what it did for Orson Welles I shall be delighted.'

The critics were less enthusiastic. Stafford Hildred, writing in the *Daily Star,* described the scene in which Sarah Greene disappeared as 'the only enjoyable moment in 90 minutes of nonsense pretending to be a proper programme'.

The *Daily Express*'s Peter Tory, meanwhile, sounded a note of caution which proved tragically close to the mark. 'Most viewers,' he said, 'would have regarded it as nonsense, which it was. A minority – the elderly, the lonely, the nervous, the gullible, the young – were terrified out of their wits.

'Television with its formidable power should be very cautious when combining apparent reality with alarming fiction. The BBC proves once again that it is out of control.'

Above: ***Parkinson, Smith and Greene pose for a publicity shot to promote*** **Ghostwatch.** ***Parkinson said later: 'If it does for my career what it did for Orson Welles I shall be delighted.'***

SCARED TO DEATH

For one family at least, those sentiments could not have been better put. Only hours after the programme went out 18-year-old Martin Denham, who had a mental age of 13, hanged himself from a tree near his home in Nottingham. His elder brother Carl told an inquest that after seeing *Ghostwatch* the teenager would not go to bed without a torch. The clanking central heating pipes had particularly worried him as it was a sound he heard regularly in his own house.

Carl said: 'He was so timid and the programme frightened him. He wanted to watch the programme so my mother sat up with him. She told him it was rubbish but he did not believe her. He was that scared by the clanging pipes of the central heating that he just went mad.'

Martin's girlfriend Rachel Young related how he had given her his most treasured possession – a crucifix – after the show went out. She was the last person to see him alive and she later told the coroner: 'He was very strange that night – the programme had affected him badly. He asked me to take his keepsake to remember him by.'

After the inquest at Nottingham in December 1992 the boy's stepfather Percy Denham made it clear he held the BBC responsible for the death. He went on: 'I think the balance of his mind was disturbed by this programme. He was a very nervous person and it upset him deeply. He became obsessed with ghosts.' Martin's mother April added: 'The BBC were totally irresponsible. Why did they say this programme was based on a real story when it was just a hoax?' Before he committed suicide Martin wrote one last note to his mum. It read: 'Mother do not be upset. If there is ghosts I will now be one and I will always be with you as one. Love, Martin.'

The BBC's solicitor Aideen Hanley, said at the time: 'Naturally the BBC and especially those connected with the making of the *Ghostwatch* programme have already expressed their sympathy in a letter sent last month by the executive producer.'

It was a grim reminder to all who work in broadcasting. As audiences go, nothing much has changed since 1938.

'IF THERE IS [*SIC*] GHOSTS I WILL NOW BE ONE AND I WILL ALWAYS BE WITH YOU AS ONE.'

COUNT ST GERMAIN

'A legend in his own lifetimes'

He fascinated the courts of 18th-century Europe, convincing kings and empresses that he was a healer, a mystic and over 150 years old. Even today there are those who claim that this enigmatic man still weaves his strange magic ...

Above: ***The court of the French king Louis XV was marked by opulence and splendour. It was thought by socialites of the day to be the very hub of Europe.***

His epitaph reads: 'He who called himself the Comte de St Germain and Welldone, of whom there is no other information, has been buried in this church'.

The epitaph could equally have read: 'Alchemist, healer, sage, wit and dandy'. Or: 'The man who claimed to have discovered the secret of eternal life'. Or should it have been: 'Charlatan'? Or simply: 'Genius'?

There were those who he was all of these ... and more.

Count St Germain was the man from nowhere who captivated the courts of Europe. He first appeared on the social scene in Vienna in 1740. At first, no one inquired too deeply as to his past – his presence was enough. He set about making an instant impression by rebelling against the brightly coloured dress of the time and opting for austere, flowing black-and-white silk clothes. He set off his sombre appearance, however, with a dazzling array of diamonds – on his fingers, his shoe buckles and his snuff box. He never used money; his pockets were always filled with diamonds. He positively glittered.

The Count St Germain was indeed a dandy. But he was graceful, charming and quick-witted. He was also, if one were to believe him, notable for another strange attribute ...

He was 150 years old!

It was a claim he made with all seriousness. It made him one of history's most fascinating men. His allusions to his own immortality drew to him the attention of Europe's intellectual and social elite. To the great French poet and dramatist Voltaire, he was 'a man who knows everything and never dies'.

But there were many other reasons why this fascinating eccentric has gone down as one of history's most puzzling men. Even now, the story of the man who called himself Count St Germain remains an unexplained enigma, perhaps because the stories he told of himself may have actually been true ...

Count St Germain was described in the scant historical records of 1740 as being a mature man, somewhere between 45 and 50 years old. He was taken under the wing of two leading socialites and dictators of fashion, Counts Zabor and Lobkowitz, the first of many to fall under the spell woven by St Germain. They installed him in a modish apartment, and through them he became well known in the social world of Vienna.

They also introduced him to a sick army general, the Marshal de Belle Isle. The nature of the general's ailment was not recorded, but it seems that after a visit from the mysterious count he was completely cured. As a token of his gratitude, Belle Isle took St Germain to Paris, then the very

THE GREAT FRENCH POET AND PHILOSOPHER VOLTAIRE SINCERELY BELIEVED THAT THE COUNT WAS 'A MAN WHO KNOWS EVERYTHING AND NEVER DIES'.

Opposite: ***Count St Germain looked young and athletic when he revealed his true age was in fact beyond 100 years. Had he really found the secret of eternal life? Or was he merely a smart fraudster?***

Above: ***After ailing Marshal de Belle Isle was miraculously cured by the count, the military man gave glowing references to him which paved his way into the highest echelons of French society.***

epicentre of cultured European life. There, he equipped himself with a laboratory, where he set to work on his alchemical studies.

In fact, the count had two pursuits. One, as old as time itself, was to discover the secret of turning base metals into gold. The other was to discover the elixir of life – 'the secrets of eternal wealth and eternal beauty', as he once described it.

A MAN OF SECRETS

It was in Paris that the strange legend of Count St Germain really began to grow. One of the first to hear of his claims that he was much older than he looked was a countess, who remarked that as a young woman in Venice in 1670, she had heard the name 'St Germain' announced by a footman. The aged countess asked St Germain if by any chance the man was his father. 'No, Madame, that was me,' he replied calmly. 'Madame, I am very old,' he told her, and said he remembered her beauty from their meeting in Venice all those years ago.

Astonished, the countess studied the charming stranger who looked not a day over 50. Then she calculated the age to which he was now laying claim: more than 120 years old!

It was but the first of the many astounding claims he was to make. He became the talk of Paris, and rumours circulating pronounced him both a genius and a devil. But in the opulent court of the Bourbon King Louis XV, the arrival of this alchemist, sage and amusing fellow caused the greatest interest.

In 1743 Count St Germain was summoned to Versailles to meet the king, whom he greatly charmed, together with the king's mistress, Madame de Pompadour. The count told them he had studied the mysteries of the Great Pyramid

in Egypt, and the secrets of Himalayan mystics and Italian occultists. Louis, completely spellbound, commissioned him to carry out secret missions for the Crown.

This may well explain how Count St Germain found himself under arrest in England. Spy fever gripped the British nation after the Young Pretender, Prince Charles Stuart, had staged the Jacobite rebellion in order to regain the Crown for his father. The Jacobites had rallied the Highland forces, taken Edinburgh and invaded England. The prince's army reached as far south as Derby but turned back, pursued by the Duke of Cumberland and his forces.

The Jacobites suffered a crushing defeat at the Battle of Culloden in 1746 and the English troops, fearful that any foreigners could be Jacobite sympathizers, started making wholesale arrests. One of the foreigners arrested was the count.

St Germain was said to have been found with pro-Stuart letters on him – reinforcing the theories of historians that he was indeed on some kind of mission for Louis. However, the unlikely explanation that they were planted on him seemed to satisfy the authorities, and he was released.

While in custody, the count had caught the attention of several prominent people, not least of them Horace Walpole, who wrote in a letter to a friend: 'The other day they seized an odd man who goes by the name of Count St Germain. He has been here these two years and will not tell who he is or whence, but professes that he does not go by his right name. He sings and

He journeyed to India to steal the secrets of the Indian mystics.

Below: ***The palace of Versailles, grand residence of the French king. At their first meeting there, the king found the mysterious count fascinating and charming.***

Above: ***Louis XV of France gave cash backing to the count in his bid to make gold from metal and gems.***

Right: ***Madame de Pompadour, the king's mistress, was equally beguiled by the smooth-talking count.***

plays on the violin wonderfully, is mad and not very sensible.'

Later that year, St Germain moved back to the city of Vienna, where he enjoyed the same adulation as in Paris. He set up another laboratory, and was feted by the Viennese court.

Between 1747 and 1756, he paid two visits to India, a land which fascinated him. From there he wrote to Louis of France that he had perfected his alchemy skills and could now 'melt jewels'. He said that the secret had been gained from Indian mystics and was guaranteed to cause a sensation on his return to Europe.

Louis had by now become so fascinated by St Germain that, upon the count's return to France in 1756, he was given another laboratory, paid for by the monarch, to enable him to carry on with his promising experiments in alchemy.

The relationship forged between the mysterious count and the king evaporated, however, after Louis sent him on a mission to Holland in 1760. Ostensibly, he was in Holland to drum up financial support for France's war effort against Britain in the conflict which became known as the Seven Years War. At The Hague, the count made an enemy of the Duc de Choiseul, Louis's foreign minister, who told his master that St Germain had taken upon himself the mantle of peacemaker and had made representations to English diplomats with a view to ending the war. The count was forced to flee from his erstwhile patron's wrath and he went briefly back to London, returning to Holland in 1764 to establish more alchemy laboratories.

AN AMAZING ODYSSEY

He stayed for two years, eventually fleeing the country with a fortune of 100,000 Dutch guilders he had amassed from manufacturing not gold but paint and dyes. He next turned up in Belgium, sporting the name Marquis de Monferrat. He remained there for only a year.

Then began an amazing odyssey across Europe and into the court of the Russian empress Catherine the Great. Such was the spell he held over Catherine, weaving tales of science and travel, that he was given special status. In 1768, when Russia had just embarked on a war with Turkey, this extraordinary man found himself advising the head of the nation's forces. And in recognition of his advice, he was given a title; the name he chose for himself was 'General Welldone'.

In 1774 Count St Germain arrived in the gracious German city of Nuremberg, raising more funds to set up yet another of

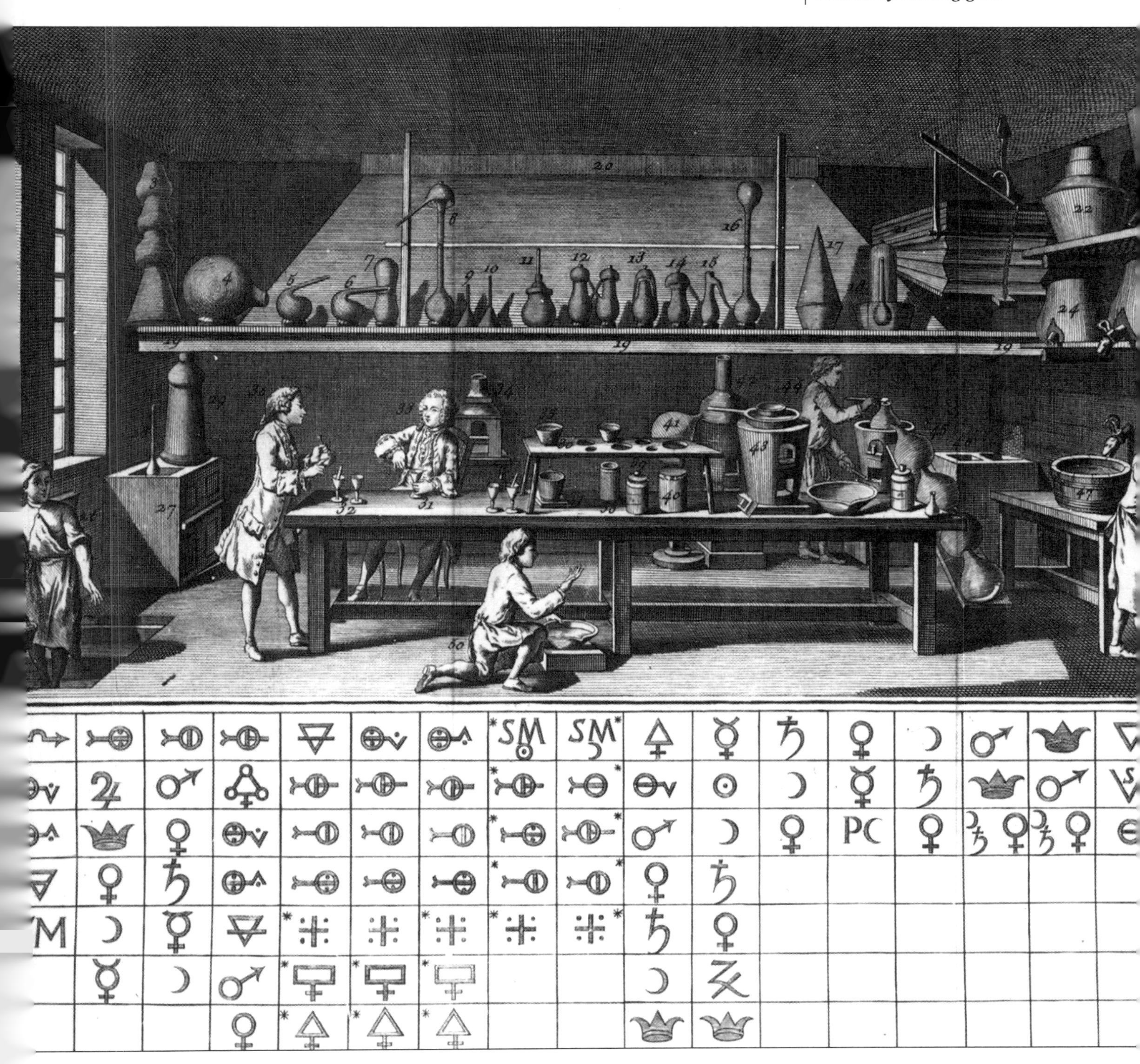

Below: ***An alchemist at work using a rich variety of symbols in his quest to find wealth beyond his wildest dreams by making gold.***

THE COUNT WARNED THE KING AND QUEEN OF THEIR IMPENDING DOOM; THEIR REFUSAL TO HEED HIM COST THEM THEIR LIVES.

his beloved laboratories so he could continue to experiment in alchemy. From here he tried lamely to curry favour once again with the very same French court from which he had had to flee.

He seemed to have remarkable foresight, for he warned Louis XVI, the old king's successor, and his wife Marie Antoinette of a 'gigantic conspiracy' which would engulf them and sweep away the old order of things. With hindsight, it is easy to recognize that this could only have been a reference to the impending French Revolution which in 1789 did indeed engulf them, and cost them their lives. They were both guillotined in the Place de la Revolution, the king on 21 January 1793 and his queen on 16 October.

During this time the count dabbled widely in the occult, freemasonry and dark arts. He approached Prince Frederick Augustus of Brunswick, claiming to be a mason. But, unbeknown to St Germain, the prince was Grand Master of the Prussian Masonic lodges and knew the claim was false. Prince Frederick became one of the few people to dismiss St Germain as a phony.

The last records of him show that he travelled to Berlin, Frankfurt and Dresden, finally arriving at what is believed to be his last resting place. He was taken under the wing of Prince Charles of Hesse-Cassel, in Schleswig, Germany, where he dazzled the prince with his worldly knowledge. His showmanship was fading, however. He was too old to play the charmer or the dandy.

Below: ***The Duc de Choiseul, who wrecked the special relationship between king and count by casting doubts on the loyalty of the latter.***

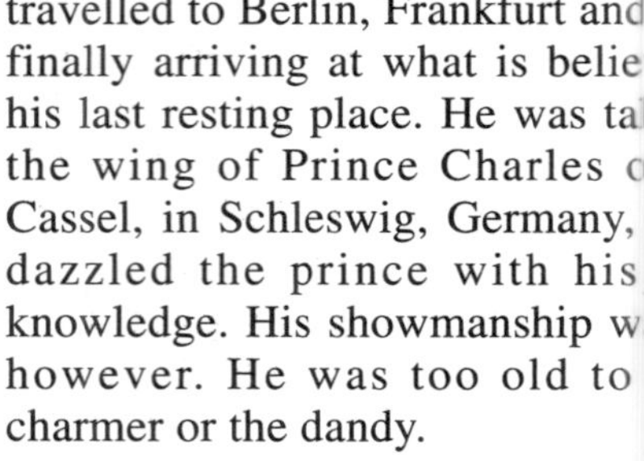

DEAD AND BURIED?

The count was by now well into his 60s, although still claiming to be many decades older. He died in 1784 and was buried in the local churchyard near his benefactor Prince Charles's home in Eckenforde. Hence the tombstone erected to his memory: 'He who called himself the Comte de St Germain and Weldone, of whom there is no other information, has been buried in this church.'

So was this to be the end of the story? Buried in a quiet corner of a country churchyard? The last resting place of a gifted adventurer, diplomat, socialite, healer and alchemist? Many think not.

Reports of sightings of the mysterious count continued to come in for another 40 years. In 1785 a group of occultists staging a conference at Wilhelmsbad reported that he had appeared before them; in 1788 he was said to be back in France warning the nobility of the revolt of the peasants set for the following year. And in 1789 he was reported to have turned up at the court of King Gustavus III of Sweden. He told a friend, Madame d'Adhemar, that he would see her five more times – and she said he was true to his word. The last time she saw him, she reported, was in 1820.

What explanation can there be for this strange figure? Was he merely a charlatan, or was he indeed a genius?

Certainly there are records in existence which say he used his charm and guile merely to make people he met part with their money. But he also had a private fund of wealth and never failed to delight in showing off the diamonds which lined his pockets. He had an excellent knowledge of chemistry, and gained great status as a healer after attending to the French Marshal de Belle Isle.

He was master of more than six foreign languages and boasted of having studied jewellery and art design at the court of the shah of Persia, as well as having learned the mysteries of the occult in faraway places. Certainly, when his knowledge was thoroughly tested by sceptics, it seemed to stand up to close scrutiny.

Emperor Louis Napoleon III was so obsessed by the legend of St Germain that he instituted a special commission to study his life and background. Ironically the findings of the inquiry board were destroyed in a fire in 1871 – something the followers of St Germain say is too uncanny to be an accident. It was an act which they considered to be the work of the count himself.

One account of the count's life says that he was born in 1710, the son of a tax collector in Italy; another that he was born in Bohemia (now part of Czechoslovakia), the son of an occultist. That, say his followers, could account for his strong bent towards the dark forces and mysticism.

A 19th-century mystic, theosophist and occultist, Madame Blavatsky, claimed that St Germain was indeed an immortal, and could be ranked alongside Buddha, Christ and others, because he enriched the world with his presence and knowledge.

In 1972 a Parisian named Richard Chanfray claimed to be Count St Germain. He went on television and, in a clever experiment involving the use of a camping stove, apparently managed to turn lead into gold. He failed to prove that he was the celebrated count. But then no one could prove that he was not!

Even today, Count St Germain attracts a dedicated, cult following. Many people believe he is still alive and will visit them again before the turn of the century. However, as to his past, where he came from, how he supported himself, and where he gained his strange powers – the mystery remains and continues to fascinate people in this modern age.

Above: ***Marie Antoinette, once the first lady of France, reduced to penury before she died at the hands of French revolutionaries. Could she have been saved if only she had listened to Count St Germain?***

ELVIS PRESLEY
Is the King dead?

The King is dead. Long live the King!' The age-old saying is charged with sinister significance with regard to Elvis Presley, the king of rock 'n' roll, whose sexy snarl inflamed teenagers and infuriated parents. For there are those who remain convinced that Elvis never died ...

Sunlight was peeping through the windows of Graceland when former beauty queen Ginger Alden awoke. Instantly she noticed the bed beside her was empty.

Calling out for her missing lover, she pushed open the bathroom door and found him curled up on the carpeted floor, his face contorted in a death mask, still clutching a book about the Turin Shroud which he had been reading. Elvis, the King, was dead.

The first person she telephoned was his tour manager Joe Esposito. There followed a 7-minute ride to Baptist Memorial Hospital where the body was attended by Elvis's personal doctor, George Nichopoulos, who kept urging the rock 'n' roll idol to breathe. But to no avail. Elvis was pronounced dead in the hospital at 3.30 pm. A subsequent postmortem revealed he died from a heart attack.

That's what happened on the day Elvis died, 16 August 1977. Or is it? Niggling

Opposite: ***In his prime Elvis Presley was an all-American boy with clean-cut good looks and greased hips. Did he pay the ultimate price for superstardom, by dying a fat-faced junkie?***

Below: ***News of Elvis's death stunned the world. British newspapers reported how his body was discovered following a heart attack.***

THE Sun

HE WAS 42 AND ALONE

KING ELVIS DEAD

ELVIS PRESLEY, the rock 'n' roll king who thrilled millions, died alone yesterday aged 42.

A massive heart attack at mansion

DAILY EXPRESS

Hospital drama of rock king

ELVIS IS DEAD

REQUIEM FOR A KING: Page 14

Sobbing

THE KING IS DEAD

Drug yearning that dragged down a legen

DAILY Mirror

BRITAIN'S BIGGEST DAILY SALE

ELVIS PRE

Daily Mail

THE GOLDEN BOY OF SPORT

Heart attack after a hard game of

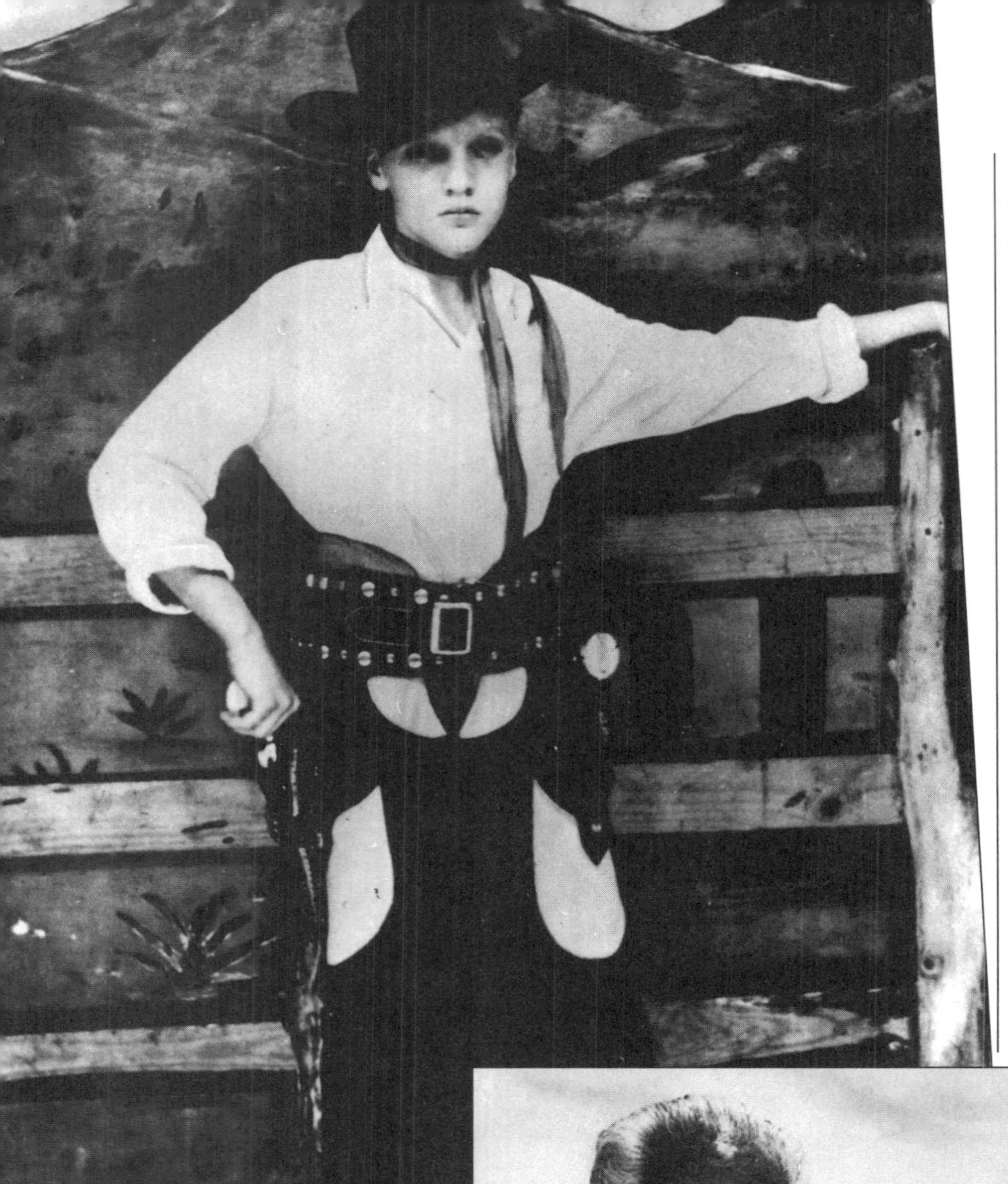

doubts were suppressed as the news sent shock waves around the world. Millions mourned for the man they worshipped. His family, especially dad Vernon and daughter Lisa Marie, were inconsolable.

SINISTER RUMOURS

But soon the rumours were abounding, some credible, some frankly astonishing. There were many who knew the King to be a bloated, drug-dependent monster who almost certainly died of an accidental overdose. Others claimed he killed himself, either in a fit of guilt about a fling with his stepbrother's wife or in order to escape a long, lingering death from cancer which had been diagnosed. Yet the official report on his death failed to mention drugs of any kind.

More sinister, there is one school of thought which claims that Elvis was murdered, most probably by vindictive Mafia men. They struck after Elvis the FBI agent helped put some of their bigwigs behind bars. Finally and most fantastically, there is the theory that Elvis didn't die at all. An actor lay in state at Graceland for

Above: ***At 13, Elvis Aaron Presley had already mastered the smouldering star look which would generate his fortune.***

Right: ***Colonel Tom Parker puts the finishing touches to a deal which would take Elvis to Pearl Harbor for a blockbusting benefit concert.***

he queues of fans to mourn, an imposter is buried in the coffin that purports to be encasing the star, and Elvis is alive, well and lurking incognito, possibly at Graceland itself. A survey carried out in 1993 discovered that as many as one in ten people believed the King was still alive.

THE HEARTACHE BEGINS

Elvis Aaron Presley was born on 8 January 1935 in East Tupelo, Mississippi, the only son of Vernon and Gladys Presley. A twin named Jesse was delivered still-born as Elvis's first cries were echoing around the room.

Mum Gladys was enchanted with the cute baby who grew up to be a handsome, happy child. So much so, she cossetted the youngster throughout his early years, the protective cloak she flung around him even extending to fetching him from school long after his friends were allowed to go-it-alone. In the end he insisted she walked behind him, ducking behind bushes and trees to cause him minimum embarrassment. Bursting with pride for her fine, charming son, she told him daily that he was as good as everybody else, despite their poverty.

His first taste of music was at the Assembly Church of God which he attended with his parents, enjoying the rhythm and melody of the gospel songs.

To celebrate his tenth birthday he went with Gladys to a local hardware store, his heart set on buying a gun. A guitar on display also caught his eye. He couldn't afford either of them but Gladys knew which she would prefer her darling boy to own. She settled the matter by offering to make up his savings with her own cash if he wanted the guitar. It was a deal. The instrument, costing less than $8, put him on the road to mega-stardom.

He began to perform gigs when he was still at school, attracting an eager following of girls even at that early age. He achieved only moderate academic success at school and as soon as he left, landed a job driving a truck paying $41 a week.

Elvis paid to make his first disc. On

Above: ***On stage, Elvis swivelled his hips and snarled with his lips, and sent hordes of female fans into a frenzy. The shock waves of his performances vibrated through America and left him bemused.***

HIS MOTHER DOMINATED HIS LIFE – SHE WAS OBSESSED WITH HER DARLING BOY AND WOULD HIDE BEHIND BUSHES TO WATCH OVER HIS SAFETY.

Above: ***By 1956 Elvis was established as the King of rock 'n' roll. His parents, Gladys and Vernon, were on hand to help sift through the piles of fan mail and gifts sent to him.***

Far right: ***The bond between mother and son was powerful. After her death, his personal life spiralled into shabby disarray.***

Opposite: ***Elvis bought Graceland, a lavish former church, with his new-found wealth as a home for himself and his immediate family. Now it is a mecca for loyal fans.***

one summer Saturday afternoon in 1953 he turned up at the Memphis Recording Studios which offered the facility to cut a record for the sum of $4, intending the tunes as a gift for his mother. There he met the woman who helped launch his career.

Assistant Marion Keisker liked what she heard when Elvis crooned 'My Happiness' and 'That's When Your Heartache Begins', two numbers originally by the Inkspots. For weeks and months afterwards she pestered her boss Sam Phillips to hear the talented teenager. It wasn't until 1954, though, that Phillips recorded 'That's All Right Mama' with Elvis on his Sun Record label. Within two days a local disc jockey had played the record 14 times in a row. It shot to number 3 in the Memphis Country and Western charts and secured a firm following of fans.

With him Elvis had a backing group, the Starlight Wranglers – later called the Blue Moon Boys – and their popularity was such that it attracted the attention of one Colonel Tom Parker. A middle-man in show business, with enough experience to spot a sure-fire winner, he cut a deal there and then which would earn him half of Elvis's cash throughout his career. In 1955 Elvis signed with RCA rec rds ar could afford to buy his mothe a pir Cadillac.

The first TV appearances on th Tomn and Jimmy Dorsey Show in Jan ary ar February 1956, spread Elvis's re utatic nationwide. He became a sensation

He was a curious mix. On the ne har he had sideburns – then consider d to b daring – wore vivid coloured clo hes an exuded the same kind of anima magnetism as his own idol Jame s Dea already dead in a car crash. Yet also h was unashamedly religious, a chu ch-go who loved his country. It was the devil i him, however, which had the reate appeal.

Colonel Parker takes credit for he hip swivelling style and alluring lip-cu l whic set hearts a-fluttering and parents blazin across middle America in the fift es. Th sexy snarl earned him as many en mies a it did fainting fans. He was denou ced b church leaders, town dignitar es, o television and radio and in the hom . But did nothing to dent his mushr omin popularity and only served to enh nce hi fame.

Chat-show host Ed Sulliva eve banned him from the show bec use h deemed Elvis was 'unfit for a family audience', but finally the phenomenon of Elvis was enough to make him change his mind. Sullivan insisted, however, that he was only filmed from the waist up. Viewing figures rocketed to 54 million, higher than those for President Eisenhower.

Police in Florida even forced the star to sing without moving. Elvis was bemused by the fuss. He told his mother: 'I don't feel sexy when I'm singing. If that was true I'd be in some kind of institution as some kind of sex maniac.'

When 'Heartbreak Hotel' was released in 1956, it confirmed his place at the top. In the same year he released a further eight singles which all stormed into the charts, among them 'Blue Suede Shoes', 'Hound Dog' and 'Love Me Tender'. Aged only 21, he had the world at his mercy.

Flexing his new-found spending power, he splashed out on Graceland, a former Christian church, in Memphis, Tennessee, painted it blue and gold and installed his parents and grandmother.

But the rock 'n' roll years had to go on ice when Uncle Sam demanded Elvis did his duty on the draft for two years. Elvis didn't mind. Standing up to 'do his share'

Right: ***Elvis enlisted for military service just like other young men of his age. But the meagre army pay packet which his fellow soldiers survived on was only a fraction of his earnings.***

Below: ***Elvis and his father mourn together after the death of their beloved Gladys. Later, Vernon could do little to curb his son's extraordinary excesses.***

like every other US boy was wonderful publicity. And it wasn't as if he was like all his fellow soldiers. He hardly needed his 478 per month army pay.

Elvis made sure his parents were close by during his basic training in Texas. He rented them a home and it was wile staying there that Gladys fell ill. She returned to Memphis where doctors discovered she had acute hepatitis and severe liver damage.

Elvis battled to win leave and rushed to her bedside, but all his fame and wealth could do nothing to save her. She died, aged 46, with her husband by her side. Vernon phoned Elvis at Graceland and he rushed to mourn over her lifeless body. The inconsolable cries of father and son cut through the night.

At her funeral Elvis collapsed three times, weeping uncontrollably and wailing: 'Oh God, everything I have is gone.'

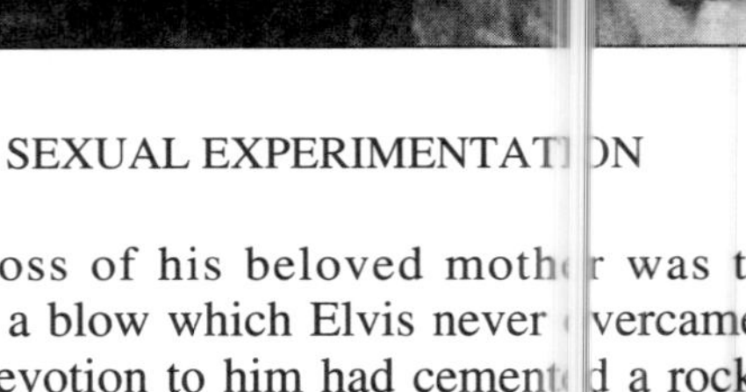

SEXUAL EXPERIMENTATION

The loss of his beloved mother was to prove a blow which Elvis never overcame. Her devotion to him had cemented a rock-solid bond but equally had stifled any emotional maturity he might have achieved too. Many blame the apron-strings tie for the sexual confusion Elvis found himself in as an adult. Certainly, on her death he seemed to lose a respect for life.

Still in the army, he was stationed in Germany and began experimenting with sex. One biographer, Albert Goldman, says that when he ate at the Lido nightclub in Paris in 1959 he ended up taking the entire chorus line of Bluebell Girls back to his hotel. This then apparently happened every night for two weeks.

Not surprisingly, he was exhausted by living life in the fast lane and was looking for a prop. He started popping pills.

Even while Elvis was in uniform, he was still churning out hit after hit, thanks to the efforts of Colonel Parker. With the army eventually behind him, he was free to pursue the career in films for which he yearned. For seven years he made an average of three films a year, none of which became known as modern classics but all of which were well supported by the fans.

As the demands made on him intensified, so did his dependency on drugs. He swallowed uppers and downers and took painkillers in pill form or by syringe: Elvis had no intention of missing out on the partying that surrounded him and his entourage, no matter how busy his schedule. He stayed with the Memphis Mafia (as his personal staff were known) in a plush Bel Air mansion which once belonged to Aly Khan and Rita Hayworth. There he hosted licentious parties night after night with scores of eager, hopeful girls outnumbering the men at the party to the tune of six to one.

Elvis took his pick; his trusted men had the best of the rest. He wasn't known for his gentlemanly behaviour towards the women he had chosen. If they upset him he was likely to throw an object at them or even toss them out of the door into the street.

Such parties became key to his very existence. He lived by night and slept all day. He had long since given up hope of shopping or eating out like other people because he would have been mobbed in the attempt.

At home in Graceland two-way mirrors were installed so he could watch other couples having sex without them realizing. Camera equipment was also moved in so the King could produce and direct his own blue movies. There was a succession of one-night stands. Elvis could pick any girl and he knew it, but soon the lure of a gorgeous, willing girl wasn't enough. Often he would pay two prostitutes to make love as lesbians to excite him sufficiently before seducing the girl he had chosen. In addition he wooed his film co-stars, beauties like Ann Margret, Tuesday Weld and Ursula Andress. From Hollywood he also dated Natalie Wood, one of the few girlfriends to be taken back to Graceland.

Outside the bedroom, his actions were increasingly bizarre too. He brandished pistols around and would shoot out a television screen if the programme he was watching annoyed him. He thought nothing of flying himself and his team 1,000 miles for a peanut butter and jelly sandwich if the mood took him. Elvis totally lost touch with reality.

Above: ***Priscilla was only 14 when she met Elvis for the first time. He soon decided he wanted to marry her and he wooed her in a transatlantic romance after seeking her stepdad's blessing.***

His other interest was football and he ran a club called Elvis Presley Enterprises. Along with everyone else in the team, he would take two uppers before going on the pitch. The pills gave them enough energy and stamina to play five games in a row.

TRUE LOVE?

Much of the cavorting happened even while he lived with Priscilla Ann Beaulieu, the woman he was later to marry. He first met her in 1959 in Bad Neuheim, Germany, when he was a GI and she a 14-year-old convent girl, daughter of a US army officer, clad in a crisp sailor suit.

Elvis liked his women petite, feminine and above all, young. His preference was for shapely legs and bottoms and virginal dress. Priscilla – or Cilla as he called her – was all of these things and more.

He asked her to spend Christmas with him in 1960 which she did. Her gift to him was a musical cigarette case which played 'Love Me Tender'; he gave her a puppy. But, of course, she had to return to her mother and stepfather in Germany.

Elvis missed her and pleaded with her

NIGHT AFTER NIGHT, HE WOULD TAKE THE ENTIRE CHORUS LINE OF GIRLS BACK TO HIS HOTEL BEDROOM.

Above: ***It seemed like a fairy-tale marriage when pretty Priscilla wed idol Elvis. In fact, she was sucked right into his twilight world of self-indulgence and infidelity and remained miserable for most of the years they spent together.***

HE WENT TO BED WITH OVER A THOUSAND WOMEN, AND FELL IN LOVE WITH A 14-YEAR-OLD CONVENT SCHOOLGIRL.

stepdad to allow her to finish her schooling in Memphis. A year later he agreed and in October 1962 Priscilla started living at Graceland and enrolled at the Catholic High School nearby. When she graduated he presented her with a Corvair.

Before her arrival, Presley had shown his stepmother a snap of Priscilla and said: 'I've been to bed with no less than 1,000 women. This is the one, right here.'

But whatever his feelings for Priscilla, he was unable to stop himself leching, both at home and in Hollywood. The couple finally married in 1967 when she reached 21, in the Aladdin Hotel, Las Vegas, followed by a honeymoon in Palm Springs, California. Nine months later Priscilla gave birth to their daughter, Lisa Marie.

Life with Elvis was no easy ride. For a start, she rarely saw him as he still lived by night and she by day. They were never alone as when they did see each other, members of the Memphis Mafia were always in evidence. And Elvis only made a modest effort to hide his series of flings from her.

'I was always on guard, always dressing to please him, always fighting for territory and fighting for what I believed in.

'I wasn't brought up to believe in divorce and when I married I thought it would be for ever.

'Everywhere I went I had women wanting him. Not just wanting him right in front of me there were things going on. It was a shock to be confronted with this at such a young age. All the time I was desperate to please,' says Priscilla now.

She believes her devotion to wifely duties almost put their child at risk. 'To Elvis I was like his kid he had raised. He used to refer to himself as Daddy.

'I gained only 9 pounds during that pregnancy and the baby was 6 pounds. I had a husband I wanted to keep. I didn't want him to look at other women, that was my motive. I don't pride myself on it and I don't recommend it. I almost starved myself. I ate only eggs during the day, apples at night, maybe one meal. I didn't drink milk and that wasn't good for the baby.'

After five years of marriage Priscilla told Elvis she had fallen in love with another and was leaving Graceland. The man in question was Mike Stone, Elvis's friend and karate instructor.

The news devastated the King. The pain was in losing one of his prized possessions to another man. He toyed with the idea of having Stone assassinated but pulled out at the last moment.

Somehow the domestic disaster gave him a new career spur and he began live performances again after a break of some seven years. The excesses with drugs, drink and women continued unabated.

Once he bought 14 Cadillacs in one night and gave them all away to friends. He spent $13,000 on handguns in one spree. His spontaneous purchases and generous gestures were without rhyme or reason.

A 20-year-old beauty queen, Linda Thompson, became his girlfriend and was showered with costly gifts, including cars and houses. But his philandering continued and she too quit the relationship. For some nine months before he died Ginger Alden was his regular girlfriend. She claimed they were engaged and had an enormous diamond to show for it.

A NEEDLE HEAD

Stepbrother and former bodyguard Rick Stanley said afterwards: 'He didn't show moderation. Not just with drugs but with anything he did. There were no half-

Left: ***Baby Lisa Marie was the child they longed for and adored. But even she wasn't enough to keep the handsome couple together.***

Below: Ginger Alden, who found Elvis's body, had been dating the King for nine months before his alleged death and claimed they were engaged.

THE FANS WHO FLOCKED TO HIS CONCERTS NEVER REALIZED THAT THEIR OVERWEIGHT IDOL WAS REDUCED TO WEARING A NAPPY.

measures. In 1972 and 1973 he started getting into needles. That's when I really started to worry, when he became a needle head. His body began to look like a pin-cushion.'

Despite his blatant misuse of drugs, there was no shortage of doctors willing to cash in on his addiction and provide a ready supply. Elvis lived on liberal helpings of drugs, junk food like hamburgers, ice cream and milk shakes washed down with whisky. Not surprisingly, his weight ballooned and he became cumbersomely large. He was so fuddled he lost control of his bodily functions. The legions of fans who still flocked to concerts never realized their idol was reduced to wearing a nappy.

In his final 24 hours it is known he visited a dentist at 10.30 pm where he had two fillings, played two hours of racquet-ball at 2.30 am and retired to bed at [illegible].30 am.

At 9 am Ginger awoke to find him still sleepless. She reported that he told her he was going into the bathroom to read a book, *The Scientific Search for the Face of Jesus*. It was there that she found him in gold pyjamas just over five hours later.

Dr Jerry Francisco, the Memphis state medical examiner, decided death was due to an erratic heartbeat, adding there were signs of advanced heart disease.

Warning bells started to ring when Elvis was buried with haste, just two days after his death. Graceland was scrupulously cleaned within hours of Elvis's death, it was later discovered, eliminating any forensic evidence. Police continually refused to probe the death.

And Dr Francisco's claim that there was no evidence of drug abuse caused many who knew Elvis to wonder. It was an open secret that he used drugs regularly – even the audiences at his concerts could detect he was under the influence. The autopsy report was declared secret for 50 years. Altogether, it smacked of a cover-up.

Later it was discovered that 2,372 uppers, 2,680 downers and 1,095 other narcotics had been prescribed to Elvis in Tennessee alone. It was surely within the bounds of possibility that he took an overdose.

Years later Elvis's doctor, George Nichopoulos, told British author John Parkes that he believed the singer was killed by the Mafia. Death was due to a fatal karate chop to the back of the head, he insists.

Why was the Mafia interested in Elvis? It is claimed he was the victim of a $900,000 fraud pulled off by an arm of the mob and helped the FBI track down the top-ranking villains. The hearings against the men involved and were due to go ahead within days of his death. Elvis's involvement in the affair had been covered up in case the Mafia sought reprisals.

In addition, Elvis was, in name at least, an FBI agent. In 1970 he visited President Richard Nixon in the White House to voice his concern about the declining moral fibre of America's youth. He dreamed of becoming an undercover cop who would help save the country from chaos and injustice. Secretly, he used the meeting to stoke up the obsession held by American

Below: ***Elvis in action in one of his last shows. On a diet of junk food and drink, his weight had soared. But dutiful fans still flocked to scream their appreciation.***

politicians that the Beatles were responsible in no small part for this, probably because the super group had decimated his popularity.

In any event, he considered himself as a top cop, absurd as it may seem when his record with drugs is taken into consideration.

A SWEATING CORPSE

Revelations that Elvis lived were made in 1989 by journalist Gail Brewer Giorgio in a book which she called *The Most Incredible Elvis Presley Story Ever Told*. Touched by Elvis's death, she wrote a fictional book about a pop star who faked his death. But when the title was suppressed after being published in 1979 she began to get suspicious. Was her made-up plot really a mirror of what had happened at Graceland?

She started some exhaustive research which she claims produced firm evidence that Elvis was alive. Hundreds of thousands of fans filed reverentially passed the coffin bearing Elvis's body in the short time before it was buried, but many left debating the unusual hairstyle and cut of the nose. Bizarrely, some even mentioned the corpse was apparently sweating. The weight of the body in the coffin was around 7 stones lighter than the bloated Elvis was when he had died, she claims.

Personal belongings like photographs and jewellery, even a plane, went missing after Elvis's death. Two days before his collapse he was heard saying goodbyes to all his most trusted members of staff. Some people believe the writing on the death certificate was actually done by Elvis himself.

There were two life insurance policies cashed in before the death. Yet a third, valuable policy has never been claimed. Fans cite this as evidence that while Elvis might fake his own death, the thoroughly upright side of his character would not allow fraud to take place in his name.

Gail Giorgio was astonished to find a man called Elvis Aaron Presley with 75 million dollars worth of stocks and shares in receipt of a security number issued by the FBI and a classified tax record.

If that wasn't enough, it is known that Elvis used the pseudonym Jon Burrows. And Gail Giorgio found a man of the same name living in Kalamazoo who not only looked like Elvis but shared the same flourishes of the pen – his handwriting was virtually identical. She also discovered Graceland was paying off credit card bills run up by a Jon Burrows as recently as 1991.

Friends recounted how Elvis was not only depressed about his advancing years and expanding figure but also at how he felt trapped by his fame. He longed to stroll down a street or around a shop like other people. A faked death would give him the new beginning he craved. Was it hard fact, mere coincidence or the product of a fertile imagination? The arguments raged on.

LONG LIVE THE KING!

Since his demise, there have been three photos produced as evidence that the King is alive, one of which was taken at Graceland. It shows a figure watching the fans trooping past the burial plot. The

Above: ***Dr George Nichopoulos, who tried frantically to revive Elvis, later said he believed the star was killed by a fatal karate chop to the back of the head.***

HAD HE ENDED HIS LIFE WITH A COCKTAIL OF DRUGS BECAUSE HE KNEW HE WAS SUFFERING FROM AN INCURABLE DISEASE?

quality of the snap is not sufficiently sharp to decide whether or not it is Elvis.

There is also the strange case of the telephone calls made sporadically in the last 15 years purporting to be from Elvis. Miss Giorgio has even received one herself. Experts believe the voice matches tapes of the King made while he was alive.

The claims have been denounced by those close to Elvis, among them Priscilla Presley who said: 'Elvis is dead and it is ludicrous to say otherwise.

'To say he is alive is a hurtful and ridiculous lie and deeply upsetting to his family, friends and fans.'

His stepmum Dee Presley agrees. She tells how he ended his life with a cocktail of drugs because he knew he was suffering from bone marrow cancer. She says her husband Vernon, Elvis's dad, found a note signed by the star detailing why he was going to commit suicide. Vernon even revealed that on the night he died he was actually reading a pornographic magazine, not a religious book as was claimed. The secrecy surrounding Elvis's death was maintained to spare Lisa Marie from knowing the truth about her degenerating dad and to keep the clean-cut image intact.

Meanwhile Elvis's stepbrother David, son of Dee by a previous marriage, revealed how Elvis was tortured with guilt after bedding the wife of another stepbrother, Billy. It was that terrible guilt which led to further drug abuse, he said.

'It haunted Elvis to the grave. He mentioned it often and it was one of the things that helped to kill him. Elvis regretted the affair from the moment he did it.

'He was worried that Billy would find out. In a short time, he cut Billy out of his life completely.

'He was plagued with paranoia and desperately lonely because he didn't know who to trust. Finally, by his own hand, he found the peace he craved for.'

Cynics simply point out that his fortunes revived dramatically on his death and have boomed ever since. Whatever the truth, it is certain that the official secrecy thrown up around the death – with files about it still under wraps for another 35 years – will continue speculation for years to come.

In 1992 Dr Vasco Smith, a political

Below: *Fans file past the grave. Yet many question whether the real Elvis lies interred here or simply a lookalike.*

Left: ***Presley's stepmum Dee claims the King killed himself rather than face the agony of death from bone marrow cancer.***

Below: Thousands pay tribute to the elaborate shrine at Graceland. Is Elvis lurking in the main house observing death rites from a window?

leader from Memphis, pledged to cut through that grey shroud of confusion and half-truths with a far-reaching investigation.

'There has been a cover up at high level and it's time the whole scandal was dragged into the open and exposed' he said

He points to how Elvis was a known drug user who had been in hospital four times in the previous two years for treatment after overdoses.

'With an intake like that, no one can ignore the possibility that Presley took a fatal overdose. It could have been accidental in his confusion or it could have been deliberate, depending on his state of mind.

'Or, as some people say, the overdose could have been administered deliberately by his enemies.

'But it is impossible to believe he wasn't full of drugs when he died. Even if it means digging Elvis out of the ground to get at the truth we have the power to do it and we certainly have the determination to do it.'

So the body of Elvis may yet be exhumed to silence the nagging doubters once and for all.

Dr Francisco continues to stand by his verdict, claiming he doesn't have the power to release the records of the post-mortem.

With the conspiracy theorists and rumour mongers still at work, Elvis, the rock 'n' roll genius of a generation, will never be able to rest in peace. dead or alive.

CLOSE ENCOUNTERS

With mounting evidence from impeccable sources, it seems absurd to deny the possibility of life in outer space. Some have risked ridicule in order to describe their ordeals; others have been cold-bloodedly silenced ...

'No one would have believed in the last years of the 19th century that this world was being watched keenly and closely by intelligences greater than man's and yet as mortal as his own; that as men busied themselves about their various concerns, they were scrutinised and studied ... '

So began H.G. Wells's *The War of the Worlds,* a novel which has long had a niche as a definitive piece of sci-fi. Yet, for a select few, those lines mean much more than mere fiction. They are a chilling reminder of ordeals that defy earthbound logic and reason. Of close encounters with alien life forms.

Strange objects in the sky have mystified human beings since prehistoric times. Every generation has been fascinated by them and as our knowledge of the Universe increases, so surely should our acceptance of the prospect of life on other planets. With more than 100,000 million stars in our galaxy alone, it seems statistically incredible to suggest the Sun is the only one which has managed to spawn life. But reports of contact with inter-planetary craft are still treated scathingly by officialdom. UFOs are for the batty, the weird, the charlatans and the dreamers.

Except that they're not. Many of the worldwide files on UFO sightings contain evidence from impeccable sources such as police officers, doctors, firemen, pilots and other trained observers. Some have risked ridicule to tell what they saw. Others have even dared to claim the ultimate in culture shock – actual contact with an alien.

FIRE IN THE SKY

One of the most fascinating cases is that of Travis Walton, an American forester, who claims he was kidnapped by aliens on 5 November 1975 and held for five days. His story is unusual because it was witnessed by six colleagues who were subsequently put under intense police interrogation on suspicion of concocting the UFO story to cover a murder conspiracy.

The gang of forestry workers had no reason to fear anyone or anything as their pick-up truck bounced down a lonely mountain track in the Apache-Sitgreave

Opposite: ***This picture, based on an eye-witness description, shows 'alien' life forms leaving their spaceship after it landed in a French lavender field.***

Below: ***This gigantic UFO was spotted over Papua New Guinea in June 1959.***

HIS 'MATES' DESERTED HIM, FLEEING THE SCENE LIKE BATS OUT OF HELL; WHEN THEY RETURNED, ASHAMED OF THEIR COWARDICE, IT WAS TOO LATE.

National Forest near Snowflake, Arizona. None could have anticipated that danger was approaching their high-spirited group. Only when it was too late would they begin to comprehend the amazing nature of the bizarre experience waiting for them around the next corner.

Walton's best friend, Mike Rogers, was at the wheel of the truck. As it rounded a corner all of the men saw a glowing, yellowish object hovering 15 feet above a clearing. Walton jumped from the truck and ran towards it to get a better view. Later he was to vividly recall the moment.

'The guys were calling me saying "get away from there, get back in the truck",' said Walton. 'I guess that egged me on. I was scared but I was showing off a bit too.' He was struck by a beam of blue light which pitched him backwards 'like a limp rag doll'. His mates in the truck fled the scene like bats out of hell [illegible]ut later, ashamed at abandoning their [illegible]olleague, they returned. The strange [illegible]raft had vanished – along with Travis Wa[illegible]ton.

During the next five days, w[illegible]th Walton still missing, the six became su[illegible]pected of killing him and dreaming up a cock-and-bull story to cover their trac[illegible]s. Police launched a massive manhunt bu[illegible] found no trace of the missing man. Then, on 10 November, Walton's sister [illegible]nswered [illegible]

Below: ***A UFO, or a strange cloud formation? This bizarre photograph was taken near the dormant volcano Mount Rainier in the US.***

ıll from a public phone in a neighbouring wn. It was Travis. He was badly shaken ıd had no idea of where he had been for e last five days. Under hypnosis he vealed: 'I know people won't believe me ıt I was in their spaceship and I met those eatures. We all saw the saucer that night. was excited and just ran towards the glow. felt no fear.

'Then something hit me. It was like an ectric blow to my jaw, and everything went black. When I woke up I thought I was in hospital. I was on a table on my back and as I focused I saw three figures. It was weird. They looked like foetuses to me, about 5 feet tall, and they wore tight-fitting tan brown robes. Their skin was white like a mushroom but they had no clear features.

'I guess I panicked. I grabbed a transparent tube and tried to smash it to use it as a weapon, but it wouldn't break. I was

Above: ***An artist put together this drawing from the reports of several eye-witnesses who saw a UFO over Exeter, New Hampshire, in 1965.***

Above: ***This object was captured on film by a Mr Barney Wayne, manager of a photographic studio in Bulawayo, Southern Rhodesia, as he drove through the north of the city. Numerous experts and press photographers pronounced it genuine.***

petrified. I wanted to attack them but they just scampered away. I knew we were in a spaceship and I felt we were moving. Then things went black again.'

He also saw what he described as a very 'human-like' figure just before blacking out again. Walton continued: 'When I woke again I was shaky. I was on the highway. It was black but all the trees were lit up because just a few feet away was the flying saucer. I was in my working clothes. I just ran and recognized a village a few miles from my home.'

The experience affected all the men badly. Three refused to go back into the woods to help the search for Walton, and Rogers lost his contract with the US Forest Service. Walton himself suffered at the hands of malicious gossips but he never changed his version of events. And 18 years later the whole, amazing story was made into a major film, *Fire in the Sky*, starring James Garner. 'If I hadn't believed Walton after talking to him for several hours I wouldn't have touched it with a barge pole,' Garner insisted later.

THE CREATURE'S BENT CLAWS AIMED THE WEAPON AT HIM AND INFLICTED TERRIBLE INJURIES.

KIDNAPPED BY ALIENS

Walton's trials were mirrored in France in 1979 when a young married man, Frank Fontaine, went missing for a wh ole wee At 4 am on 26 November he w s helpi two friends load a van with c othes f Gisors market near Paris whe they a spotted a 'bright and twirli g ligh descending nearby. Fontaine dro e towar where it seemed likely the lig ht wou land. It was the last anyone saw of him f a week.

One of Fontaine's friends des cribed h disappearance in these words: When came out Frank's van was 2(0 metr away. It was covered in a bright l ght, lik halo surrounding it. Three ot er brig lights were nearby. Then they all converg on the van.' As the frightening alo lift into the night sky, the frie d and companion rushed forward to fi d the v empty. The engine was still runni g and t headlights were on.

When Fontaine turned up, t exact 4 am the following week, he c aimed had blacked out in the bright ligh s and h awoken at the same spot, assumi g the v had been stolen. He had no i ea tha whole week had passed.

The victims in most recor led UF abduction cases are returned nharme apart from the psychological sc rs and inevitable amount of ridicule. Howev there are exceptions and o the fe

Above: ***A scene from the most famous UFO movie of all –*** **Close Encounters of the Third Kind** ***– shows investigator Dr J. Allen Hynek trying to solve the puzzle.***

documented cases that exist it seems one danger of a close encounter is a large dose of radiation. The symptoms are usually clear cut … and difficult for UFO sceptics to easily explain away.

TOO CLOSE FOR COMFORT

One such case occurred in Finland on 7 January 1970 when two friends out on a skiing trip spied a UFO which left them suffering from appalling physical side-effects for around two months. Aaron Heinonen and Esko Viljo had stopped to admire a few stars pinpricking out of a cold sunset when they suddenly spotted a much brighter light emerging quickly out of the dusk towards them. Surrounded by a thin cloud of smoke was a circular saucer-shaped object with a dome above.

Abruptly, a beam of light fired down from the spaceship to the ground. Heinonen later recalled: 'Suddenly I felt as if someone had seized me from the waist and I took a step backwards. Then I saw the creature, standing in a beam of light, with a black box in its hands. From an opening in the box there was a yellow, pulsating light. The creature was about 35 inches high with very thin arms and legs. Its ears were small and close in to the head and the face was like wax. Its fingers were like bent claws around the box.'

Heinonen was hit by a blast of light from the mysterious box and the pair were covered in a strange red-grey mist. Then, as suddenly as it had arrived, the beam of light and the spaceship were gone.

Heinonen was paralysed down his right side and his friend had to virtually carry him two miles to their home. 'For two months afterwards I felt ill,' he said later. 'My back was aching and all my joints were painful. My head ached and I had to vomit. When I went to pee, the urine was nearly black – it was like pouring coffee onto the snow.'

Viljo suffered a reddened and swollen face. He became incoherent and absent-minded. Paul Kajanoja, one of the doctors who examined the two men, commented: 'The symptoms are like those after being exposed to radioactivity. Both men seemed sincere. I don't think they made the thing up. I am sure they were in a state of shock when they came to me. Something terrible must have frightened them.'

A DIAMOND ON FIRE

Three other victims of 'UFO radiation' caused enormous headaches for the US government during the early eighties. Their account has an extraordinary ring of truth about it, partly because of the sheer detail it contained and partly because of the inexplicable, and indisputable, side effects the three suffered. No doctor has ever been able to explain what caused the conditions which later dogged their lives.

Vickie Landrum, her grandson Colby Landrum and their friend Betty Cash were driving towards Dayton, Texas, on 29 December 1980 when young Colby saw a huge glowing object at tree-top height above the lonely forest road in front of them. Frightened, but curious, they stepped out of the car to get a closer look.

At that time the object was still some

Above: ***The US military gets very edgy when unidentified intruders such as this fly into American airspace. This photo was snapped by nurse Ella Louise Fortune near the Hollman USAF base, New Mexico, in October 1957.***

three miles away although as they drove cautiously towards it they realized it was heading their way. Verging on panic now, they accelerated, but the UFO – many times bigger than their automobile – stopped directly in front of them, hovering above the road. They glimpsed a conical burst of flame from beneath the craft and Vickie recalls screaming: 'Stop the car or we will be burned alive.' Every time the flames belched out the object would rise up several metres, only to gradually fall again when the blast petered out. For all the world it looked like a sci-fi scene of an alien craft in trouble or, as Vickie would assert later, 'like a diamond on fire'.

The UFO seemed to be made of an aluminium-type metal and was lit so brightly it turned night (it was around 9 pm) into day. Its diamond shape had blunted points and hazy blue lights ringed its centre. Occasionally it made a beeping sound and Cash and the Landrums recall worrying that it would set the trees alight if it moved off the road.

The three of them got out of the car to get a better look, but after a couple of minutes Vickie bowed to her grandson's plea to return inside. Betty, however, stayed put. Her eyes were captivated by the amazing machine in front of her and her senses were somehow dulled to the burning heat.

THE DOCTORS WERE BAFFLED AND WORRIED: MEDICAL TEXTBOOKS ARE LIGHT ON ADVICE FOR TREATING CONDITIONS CAUSED BY ALIEN BEINGS.

It was only when she became conscious of one of her rings burning into her skin that she snapped out of the reverie. Vickie's frantic calls for her to get back in the car were heeded. Even then there was a moment's hesitation. The handle of the door was too hot to touch by hand. Betty had to use her leather coat for protection before she could grip it.

By now the UFO was heading away … but almost immediately a new puzzle emerged. The sky suddenly filled with the sound of helicopters – 23 in all – which, as Betty put it later, 'seemed to rush in from all directions … it seemed like they were trying to encircle the thing'.

The three of them reached a larger road which enabled them to keep track of the chase. Later their descriptions helped experts identify the choppers as Chinooks (which have distinctive double rotor blades) and small, fast-attack helicopters similar to a Bell Huey. The pilots appeared to be in an erratic trail formation, though one group had managed to shadow the UFO fairly closely and was clearly illuminated in its light.

After a close encounter lasting 20 minutes Betty turned onto another highway and headed home to Dayton. She dropped off Vickie and Colby and returned to her own house, where a friend and her children were waiting. She didn't mention the UFO. Probably she was in shock. She was certainly feeling very, very ill.

Of the three witnesses Betty had easily the longest exposure to the craft's energy source. As the night wore on her skin turned red, as though she had a bad dose of sunburn. Her neck puffed up, blisters burst onto her scalp, face and eyelids. She was violently sick throughout the night and by morning was close to a comatose state. Vickie and Colby later presented themselves to doctors with similar symptoms, though less severe.

The local hospital began treating all three for burns. No one had told them about a possible UFO involvement and even if they had, the medical textbooks are light on advice for treating conditions caused by alien beings. The doctors were both baffled and worried. Betty's swollen appearance, together with the bald patches spreading across her scalp, had changed her features so drastically that visitors failed to even recognize her. All the doctors could suggest was that she had suffered a massive dose of some kind of electromagnetic radiation.

OFFICIAL COVER-UP?

The interrogation of all three witnesses, in which each was questioned separately, showed their recollections to be remarkably consistent. Not only did they notice the same features on the UFO, they also provided similar sketches identifying the choppers as Chinook CH-47s. Yet this caused a new problem. Of the 400 or so helicopters running commercial flights in the Houston area, none was twin-rotor. And the nearest army base, Fort Hood near Killeen, Texas, said it had no aircraft anywhere near Houston on the night of 29 December.

Hood's spokesman Major Tony Geishauser observed: 'I don't know of any other place around here that would have had that number of helicopters. I don't know what it [the UFO] could be, unless there's a super-secret thing going on and I wouldn't necessarily know about it.' Other air bases, further away, were contacted by the media. All denied knowledge of any large-scale helicopter movements on 29 December.

Interestingly, on the previous day at least one helicopter had been sent to investigate UFO activity above Ohio county, Kentucky. Dozens of residents reported seeing strange lights in the sky and several witnessed the services helicopter flying above them. Yet, once more, the military denied having any choppers flying that evening.

It was not as if Betty, Vickie and Colby's story lacked corroboration. An off-duty cop and his wife driving near Huffman, Texas – close to the point the UFO first appeared – reported seeing a major movement of CH-47s. And oilman Jerry McDonald told of seeing a UFO from his back garden. 'It was kind of diamond-shaped and had two twin torches that were shooting brilliant blue flames out the back,' he said.

Investigations into the Huffman incident continue to this day. One group specializing in the probing of unusual phenomena, the Houston-based Vehicle Internal Systems Investigative Team (VISIT), offered two mind-boggling theories.

The first is that the craft was a UFO that had got into trouble. It was flying on some kind of emergency energy system which resulted in the belching of blue flames. It

Below: ***The clearer the photo, argue the sceptics, the more likely it is to be faked. This picture, taken on 16 June 1963 at Peralta, New Mexico, is among the clearest of any UFO snaps on record.***

had been tracked on radar and the military guessed it could crashland. The CH-47s were therefore ordered in as troop carriers to cordon off the area from inquisitive eyes while the single rotor choppers were attack craft ready to offer such protection as they could give. When the UFO solved its propulsion problem it headed for the coast and was escorted along the way.

One factor in support of this theory is that those experiencing close encounters with UFOs rarely suffer any personal injury. The suggestion is that if there is anyone out there they are friendly beings. They intended no harm to befall Vickie, Betty and Colby but could not control their radiation emissions.

The second theory holds that on the night of 29 December the military had 'road tested' a top-secret new invention. The 'alien craft' could in fact have been some kind of weapons system, an electronic jamming device or a revolutionary power plant. It could have been slung below the belly of one of the helicopters and all personnel involved would have donned protective clothing. The injuries Betty received could have been the result of a mega-strong microwave power pack or exposure to tiny droplets of some revolutionary fuel.

The US government, however, has always adamantly refused to admit it owns the helicopters, even though they were seen by six, separate, reliable witnesses. In view of the fact that no one will admit to authorizing the chopper excursion, the obvious conclusion is that a highly classified operation was going on that night.

Vickie and Betty later sued the American government for $20 million but the case was dismissed on the grounds that the military had no such object in its possession. The dilemma for the authorities was: if the flying craft was American, then the case should proceed. If it was not, and the court ruled it was not, then exactly who was transporting a dazzling, diamond-shaped, flame-belching machine across the night skies of Texas?

The whole bizarre affair has one tantalizing postscript. In April 1981 Colby Landrum saw a CH-47 landing in Dayton. The sight brought back memories of the Huffman incident and he became increasingly distressed. To try and get him to face up to his fears, Vickie took him to the site of the landing and introduced herself to the pilot. Without prompting, he told her he had been to the area previously to check out a UFO reported to be in trouble. When Vicki explained her interest he suddenly became nervous and refused to talk further. They were politely invited to leave the CH-47.

The VISIT group later tracked down this pilot and questioned him. He confessed to knowing about the Huffman incident but emphatically denied he had ever been in the region on that fateful December night. To date, none of the helicopter pilots involved has ever broken ranks and told what he knows.

SOMETHING VERY ODD

Although what happened at Huffman was exceptional, even by the standards of the most ardent ufologist, it is by no means unusual for UFOs to have a physical effect on everyday objects. Stories of cars malfunctioning close to strange flying lights in the sky are legion and many witnesses will tell of engine failure, bizarre static noise on the radio, rough running, impossible readings on their instruments and light failure. Occasionally a vehicle's internal wiring is completely blown out.

Drivers often report inexplicable heat or vibration or the feeling that they have driven into a field of static electricity. Some even talk of smells that are, quite literally, alien to them. Yet in most cases once the UFO concerned has passed on everything returns to normal.

One of the best documented examples of this phenomenon again happened in Texas. (It should be noted that Mexico appears to have more than its fair share of UFO activity and perhaps some of this occasionally spills across the border.) On the night of 2 November 1957 Patrolman A.J. Fowler was on the night shift at Levelland police headquarters. Up until 11 pm it was the usual routine of investigating break-ins, pulling in drunks and calming down the odd wild party. Suddenly everything changed. Patrolman Fowler would remember that shift for the rest of his life.

Soon after 11 pm he took a call from a

motorist called Pedro Saucedo who had been out driving four miles west of the city with a friend. Pedro sounded excited, panicky even, as he relayed how a brilliant yellow and white cigar-shaped object passed above his truck at very high speed. As the UFO crossed the road Pedro's headlights died and his engine failed. He had clambered out for a better look but was immediately crushed by a searing heat and found himself flat on the ground.

Seconds later the headlights flickered back into action and the engine started without any problem. Pedro had never seen anything like it. Was it a flying saucer? What were the police going to do about it? Had anyone else reported seeing something similar? Officer Fowler made what he judged to be the right calming noises and rang off. He didn't feel inclined to call out the National Guard. Probably the guy had had a few too many, seen a meteor and let his imagination take over. Either that or he was just a good old-fashioned nut. There were always plenty of those for the night roster to handle.

Then another call came an hour later. This time a motorist travelling around eight miles east of Pedro – on the UFO's apparent flight path – reported coming across a bright, 200-foot-long egg-shaped device which had touched down right in the middle of the road. As the car drew near its engine had stalled and the headlights failed. But this driver could see the surrounding countryside clearly in the light of the craft.

Above: ***A UFO over Milan in 1962? Or an over-productive imagination at work? This drawing was artist Gaspare de Lama's portrayal of his sighting.***

UNTIL 11 PM IT WAS THE USUAL ROUTINE OF INVESTIGATING BREAK-INS, PULLING IN DRUNKS AND CALMING DOWN THE ODD WILD PARTY. SUDDENLY EVERYTHING CHANGED.

When he opened his door it took off, quickly toned down the illumination and merged into the night sky.

Now Fowler was curious. Was this some kind of stunt? Were some colleagues playing him up? If so they were playing with fire. The cops took a dim view of juvenile behaviour like that. He was just convincing himself that practical jokers or unusual weather phenomena were to blame when a third call came in. Neville Wright was heading towards Levelland when his car's ammeter began flickering, the lights cut out and the engine spluttered to a halt. He'd checked under the hood but could find nothing wrong. Then he'd spotted the brilliant stationary light on the road ahead.

Within the space of the next hour four more positive sightings came in, all from good witnesses. A fire chief told of a red light that passed close to him and temporarily seemed to drain his car's battery. A sheriff and his deputy radioed that they had seen an extremely unusual red flying object. Patrolman Fowler was by now convinced something very odd was happening in the skies above Texas that November night.

To this day no scientist has been able to explain the string of vehicle electrical failures, let alone the UFO itself. Unproven theories have it that a super-powerful electromagnetic field was generated by the saucer, that its microwaves heated up the engine's vital electrical components or that refined ultra-violet light caused current to short and stray. One suggestion is that microwave radiation can interfere with tungsten headlamps to impose a massive and sudden drain on the battery. None of these ideas has ever been put to the test, at least not publicly. If the US government knows more, it is staying silent.

The role of governments in the UFO debate is itself fascinating. Exactly what do the major powers know? If alien cultures have indeed reached planet Earth why the big cover-up? Are our politicians really worried that we're all going to throw ourselves off the nearest bridge? Or is it that privately, at least, many in government accept that some kind of UFO activity has been going on for years? To admit it would be a political minefield. Once you admit something you have to explain it to the voters.

Below: ***Police probe the remnants of a 'crashed UFO'. Civil engineer Barney Barnett's discovery in the New Mexico desert remains one of the world's great mysteries.***

SOVIET SKULDUGGERY

Thankfully, some governments do take a less secretive attitude. In June 1952 six Norwegian army jets on training flights over the remote Spitzbergen islands reported debris across a mountainous area close to the Hinlopen Straits. Hours later a team of investigators was on site and allied powers in the West were alerted. Was this Soviet skulduggery at work? Perhaps a missile on test or some kind of revolutionary aircraft?

The wreckage was certainly an eye-opener. There were 46 holes in the object's rim which could have been linked to its propulsion methods. Of occupants there was no sign. The press jumped on the story but most editors tended to follow the official line that the crashed craft was a failed piece of Soviet hardware. It was not until 1955 that a senior Norwegian army officer revealed the truth.

Colonel Gernod Darnbyl of the Norwegian General Staff, said: 'The crashing of the Spitzbergen disk was highly important. Although our present scientific nowledge does not permit us to solve all ɿe riddles I am confident that these ɜmains from Spitzbergen will be of utmost nportance. Some time ago a misunder-tanding was caused by saying that this isk probably was of Soviet origin. We ʼish to state categorically that it was not uilt by any country on Earth. The ıaterials used in its construction are ompletely unknown to the experts that ɔok part in the investigation.' He revealed ıat US and British scientists had been iven access to the remains. To this day ıeir reports have never been released.

Another government which takes the pen-book approach is that of France, ʼhich has some of the world's most ɔphisticated defence technology. In 1974 ıe French defence minister Robert Galley ıade an astonishing statement in which he ɜemed to suggest that UFO sightings had ecome of enormous concern to his overnment. He told a radio interviewer: 'It irrefutable that there are things today that re inexplicable, or poorly explained ... I ıust say that if your listeners could see for ıemselves the mass of reports coming in om aircraft pilots, from patrol police and rom those charged with the job of onducting investigations ... then they ʼould see that it is all pretty disturbing.'

Certainly officialdom has started to lacken the chains of secrecy around UFO ocumentation. Spain released its files in 976, Americans were given access to the o-called Blue Book project in 1977, rance set up a government-backed UFO tudy group in the late seventies, while ustralia went public on its records in 981. Even Britain, which still has one of ıe most secrecy-obsessed governments in ıe world, has relaxed its guard a little. In ıe early seventies the UK agreed to keep a ermanent record of UFO sightings (prior ɔ then all reports were destroyed after five ears) and in 1982 it was decided that uestions from the public about specific ncidents could be answered.

The problem here, of course, is in the hrasing of the question. Asking a Vhitehall mandarin whether a UFO which rashed in hills above Bala, north Wales, in he mid-seventies contained any evidence f alien life forms will make you none the viser. The civil servant will, truthfully, eply that there was no such evidence – even if there were characteristics about the wreckage which could not be explained by conventional science. Similarly, too vague a question will elicit too vague an answer.

Some hard evidence of UFOs, though, does seem to exist. On 2 July 1947, at about 9.50 pm, a Mr and Mrs Wilmot of Roswell, New Mexico, were enjoying the evening dusk when they suddenly saw a glowing object travelling quickly north-east towards the neigbouring town of Corona. The next day civil engineer Barney Barnett, of Socorro, New Mexico, was working out in the desert 250 miles west of Roswell. A metallic object glinting in the sun caught his eye and he drove over to check it out. He thought it might be a crashed aircraft. What he found was a metallic craft 30 feet in diameter ... but it seemed no earthly hand had fashioned it. Around it lay dead bodies, bodies with very small eyes and very large heads and bereft of hair. They were wearing grey body suits.

Minutes later a group of archeological students working nearby arrived to take a look. They were equally astonished and, like Barnett, concluded that this was perhaps the first hard evidence of alien life. At least, this is how the story goes.

Apparently the army then turned up and cordoned off the entire area. Barney and the students were told it was their patriotic

The impossible had happened: at last there was hard evidence of alien life.

Above: ***Phone home! A scene from Spielberg's* E.T.** ***Public fascination with UFOs helped it become one of the biggest Hollywood blockbusters of all time.***

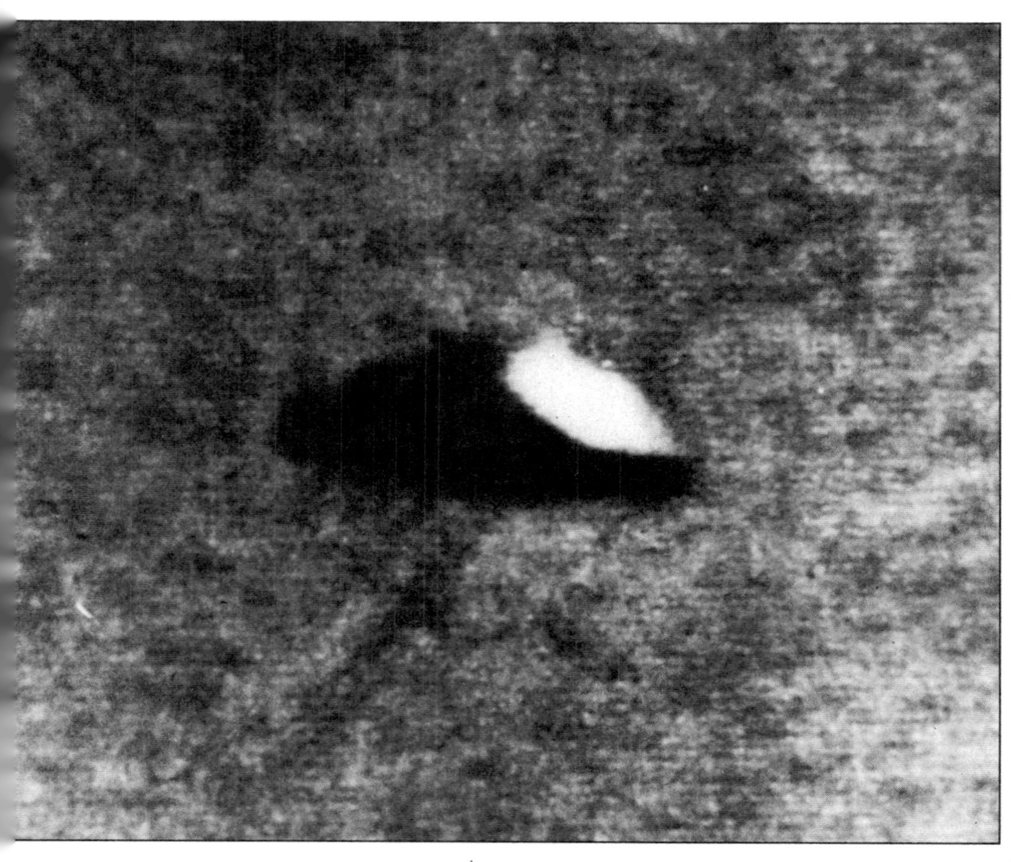

Above: ***A trick of the light or an alien spaceship? This photo was taken by a postman on his rounds in 1955.***

THE SCEPTICAL BRITISH CORONER WAS FORCED TO CONCEDE THE POSSIBILITY OF ALIEN FORCES AT WORK.

duty to reveal nothing of what they had seen. In 1947, with the Cold War looming fast, orders like that from the military certainly carried weight with the American public.

But before he died Barney did talk – to a close group of friends. Gradually the story leaked out and several journalists took a keen interest. They could find no reason for Barney's friends to lie, neither could they unearth anything about his past character which suggested he'd be the kind of man who enjoyed hoaxing others. Was he hoaxed himself? Were the students pranksters who just liked to be as elaborate as possible? If so, they were truly convincing. Barney's account suggested a great deal of military hardware was brought onto the crash site together with the soldiers to operate it. The students, sadly, were never traced.

SEXUAL FANTASY

The Roswell incident does have some factors in common with close encounters elsewhere. Grey body suits and small eyes, for instance, formed part of the description of aliens given by a Brazilian farmer called Antonio Villas Boas. He encountered them when they landed in his field. His accou remains the most incredible and far-fetch of all … because he claims to have had s with one of the extra-terrestrials.

One night in 1957, Boas had bee ploughing the fields with his brother wh he noticed a ball of red light in the sk above. The following night the red ball w still there and, as he was alone this time, grew scared and decided to drive his tract away. Boas claims the red ball then land in front of him and he was captured by fi entities wearing grey, tight-fitting suits a helmets which revealed only their sma blue eyes.

He says he was led onto the spacesh where he was forcibly stripped and a thic transparent liquid was spread over his ski Then he was marched into a small roo where a blood sample was taken leaving small scar (the scar was later verified those investigating Boas's claims. Half hour later a beautiful female alien walk in completely naked. 'Her body was mo beautiful than any I had ever seen befor said Boas. The alien then embraced hi and forced him to copulate with her. S took place a second and then a third tim though Boas was vague about the interva between each. The alien then seemed suggest his seed was wanted for breedi stock – she pointed at her belly and th the sky.

Later, after Boas was returned to h field, he consulted a doctor. Bur seemingly caused by radiation were fou on parts of his skin. However most of t locals contended his account was pu fantasy.

THE MOST MYSTERIOUS DEATH

Quite often incidents such as this a dismissed purely on the grounds that a information relating to them has bee gleaned by journalists: reporters after good story are not, it is argued, going worry too much about over-egging th pudding. Yet some investigations into UF activity are carried out openly b responsible, naturally cautious authoritie and they don't come much more sceptic or cautious than your averag Britis coroner.

One such coroner is James Turnbull, Yorkshire, England. In the mid-eighties h

ook charge of an inquest touching the death of a quiet Polish exile, Zygmunt Adamski, who vanished one night while en oute to buy potatoes from his local shop in Leeds, Yorkshire. He didn't drink and he had no known enemies. But he was found dead five days later on top of a coal tip 30 miles away near the railway station at Todmorden. Adamski was half-naked but his body was spotlessly clean as though he had just stepped out of a shower. The smooth sides of the coal tip indicated nobody had tried to climb it.

Parts of the body were burned with corrosive substances which scientists were unable to identify. Tests showed the deceased had succumbed to a heart attack eight or ten hours before his body was dumped. The local rumour-mongers had no doubts: Adamski had been scared to death by a flying saucer.

If such talk was dismissed as nonsense by the authorities they quickly changed their tune. One policeman first called to the scene of the 'crime' told how he had seen what looked like a flying saucer only hours before the body was discovered. PC Alan Godfrey, a down-to-earth father of two children, said he had been on night duty when he encountered the UFO on a lonely road. It was the size of a bus and floated about 5 feet from the ground. The bottom half was spinning and he could see rows of windows around a dome. But when he tried to alert his station to what he was seeing he couldn't. His walkie-talkie wouldn't work.

Such facts as these were laid before Coroner James Turnbull. His comments at the inquest speak volumes because he was a neutral and expert assessor of evidence.

'This is quite the most mysterious death I have ever investigated,' he said. 'As a coroner I cannot speculate. But I must admit that if I was walking over Ilkley Moor tomorrow and a UFO came down I would not be surprised.

'I might be terrified ... but not surprised.'

Above: ***We are not alone. Jillian Guiler (played by Melinda Dillan) and son Barry (Cary Cuffey) are transfixed by the bright lights of a UFO above their home. Scenes like this from* Close Encounters *gave the UFO debate a new edge.***

JIMMY HOFFA
‘A tainted folk hero’

Jimmy Hoffa was a small man with a gigantic lust for power. Rough and tough, he fought his way up from the bottom of the heap and didn't care who he trampled on or how many enemies he made ...

The day that Jimmy Hoffa vanished, a nation held its breath. Was this just another wild stunt by the charismatic champion of the American working man? Or had the 'little guy' breathed his last?

Jimmy Hoffa left his home on the outskirts of Detroit on 30 July 1975 and was never seen again, alive or dead. Ever since in the minds of the ordinary people who had followed his amazing exploits – sometimes with admiration, sometimes with awe, but often with horror – there has been a huge fascination as to his fate.

For Hoffa's firebrand exploits were the stuff of legend, lovingly reported by the media. He was that curiously American animal: a tainted folk hero.

He had fought the Kennedys, courted the Mafia, stolen workers' millions, been imprisoned, courted Richard Nixon, done battle with the Mafia, won back the workers and split the unions. And then he was suddenly gone.

Ironically, James R. Hoffa was christened with the middle name 'Riddle'. And the riddle of his disappearance has intrigued America and confounded the authorities. The FBI is still actively investigating the Hoffa disappearance, still conducting the biggest manhunt in its history. The US Justice Department still has a 'live' casefile on him.

But the authorities never did make a single arrest in the case nor did they turn up any evidence of Jimmy's body. So what happened? Was he turned into glue? Ground up in a mincer? Compacted in a garbage plant? Cemented into a bridge? Squashed inside a junked car? Fed to Florida's alligators? Or could he perhaps still be alive?

HOOKED ON POWER

Born 14 February 1913, from his humble beginnings Hoffa rose to the top with the help of the underworld. He made little pretence of being a nice guy. In the rough-and-ready Depression era, he fought his way from a job as a loading dockworker to become president in 1957 of America's largest and most powerful trades union.

His power turned the disorganized International Brotherhood of Teamsters into a major force. Anything that involved cartage was operated by the Teamsters, descendants of the stagecoach drivers, pony expressmen and muleteers of pioneer days. Even the Michigan State Police joined Hoffa's union.

When he was attorney general, Robert Kennedy grilled Hoffa mercilessly about

Opposite: ***Cunning, controversial, conniving. Yet nevertheless Hoffa, seen here giving evidence at a rackets' hearing, was a hero to thousands and mourned by many as America's mouthpiece for the working man.***

Below: ***Teamsters pickets demonstrate solidarity outside a trucking firm in dispute with its drivers.***

Above: ***There was no love lost between Hoffa and Robert Kennedy. Hoffa even threatened to sue Kennedy after being branded a communist.***

IN JAIL HE BOASTED HE'D NEVER READ BOOKS – JUST THE CONTRACTS HE'D TAKEN OUT ON OTHER PEOPLE'S LIVES.

his strongarm tactics. Employers bought union peace and stability, plus a share of the pension fund rip-off, and all it cost them was their integrity.

He liked to boss other people about. At Lake Orion, neighbours didn't like to stop and chat with Jimmy for long because they would get a rake shoved in their hand with instructions to work!

Hoffa was a devoted family man with a puritanical streak. But he still went in for diamond cufflinks, convertible cars, top-line hotels and furnishings – as long as the Teamsters picked up the tab.

How much of a crook was Hoffa? He boasted he had 'a record as long as your arm': 23 arrests dating back to 1937, the year he married Josephine Pozywak. However, he had been fined only twice (the first time for $10, the second for $1,000) and he had never been to jail. That changed on 4 March 1964 when he was sentenced to eight years on two out of three counts of jury tampering. Seven weeks later he was back in court for a 3-month trial that ended with him being given an additional 5-year sentence for mail fraud, milking the Teamsters' principal pension fund of $2 million.

He went to prison in 1967 after his appeals had all been lost. Even behind bars, however, he was still a hero with a loyal, almost fanatical, trade union following. America has always rooted for the little guy, and Hoffa was tiny. Five foot 5, never weighing more than 13 stone, he did daily push-ups in prison. He boasted that he had never read a book ('I read contracts, not books') but behind bars he read ten books a month.

Before going down, Hoffa had arranged for a weak caretaker deputy, his cohort from the local Detroit branch, to become the union's titular head. Frank Fitzsimmons turned out to be more tenacious once he became president.

Hoffa served only 58 months of his 13-year sentence. Then, in December 1971 when the Federal Parole Board had turned down his third parole appeal, President Nixon suddenly commuted his sentence. He was free. But there was a catch in the Nixon deal: Hoffa was barred from union activities until 1980 – which just happened to coincide with the end of Fitzsimmons's term of office.

Hoffa cried loudly that the president had betrayed him; he claimed Nixon and Fitzsimmons had conspired against him in secret. Why would the president of the USA get involved at all? For money, said the Phoenix-based *Arizona Republic* newspaper, which obtained an incriminating document from law enforcement officials in 1979. The newspaper said that Nixon got half a million dollars out of Mafia funds.

An alleged 19-page mob diary threw new light on the links between criminals, unions and politicians. The diary was handed to the FBI by convicted hitman Gerald Denono, who said he stole it from another mobster, bagman Edward 'Marty' Buccieri, who was murdered in 1975. The document, which covered a 15-month period from 1972 to 1973, itemized $2

illion in illegal financial transactions. The iary named Nixon aides Bob Haldeman, harles Colson and John Ehrlichman.

Hoffa allegedly promised Nixon ndorsement by the Teamsters and other nions in the 1972 election. Nixon needed is backing since he had already angered e unions in 1971 with his price control easures.

Once he was out of prison, Hoffa's ission was therefore to wrest control of e Teamsters away from his one-time rotégé Fitzsimmons, who was now firmly ntrenched and obstinate.

Hoffa would tell people: 'I know the nion business upside-down around and ver. The members are interested in how any bucks they can make. I get them for em.'

There was a split in the trade union ranks and the ensuing feud was violent. Detroit Teamsters official Dave Johnson was beaten up, his office was machine-gunned and his boat was blown apart. Union organizer Eugene Paige's house was blown up. Another official, George Foxburgh, was hit by a shotgun blast and lost an eye. Fitzsimmons's son Dickie, a local branch official, was drinking in a bar when his Teamsters-owned car exploded in a ball of flame outside. This was on 10 July 1975 – exactly three weeks before Hoffa vanished.

It was trade union civil war.

Hoffa was interested purely in power, not riches. He already had a $1.7 million pension pay-off that he'd taken in a cash lump sum, and he had other business interests. He had, of course, served time for theft of an enormous sum from the

Above: ***More than 10,000 truckers, warehousemen and taxi drivers crammed into Madison Square Gardens in 1960 to hear Hoffa crusading against a new labour reform law.***

Teamsters' pension fund, Yet he still enjoyed the personal loyalty of 2.2 million members of America's most powerful union.

Then he disappeared.

AN UNDERWORLD RUBOUT

Late in the afternoon of 30 July 1975, 62-year-old Hoffa left his ritzy suburban home in Lake Orion, 45 miles north of Detroit.

He was wearing a blue sports shirt and dark trousers. He was going to the Machus Red Fox restaurant in Bloomfield township.

THEY'D BEEN ALLIES – AND THEN SOMETHING HAPPENED TO TURN THEIR FRIENDSHIP INTO BITTER HATRED.

Hoffa is believed to have been abducted from outside the restaurant – the victim of an underworld rubout. But by whom? And why?

Hoffa had told his wife that he had a dinner date at the restaurant with two men: Anthony Giacolone, a Detroit hoodlum, and Anthony Provenzano, known as Tony Pro, a soldier in the influential Mafia crime family of Vito Genovese. Giacolone was a simple hood, but Provenzano, a former amateur boxer, was more than just a Genovese soldier. He was a local leader of the Teamsters in Union City, New Jersey.

Tony Pro and Hoffa bore a fierce hatred for one another. They had been friends and allies, but after a joint spell in the Federal Penitentiary at Lewisburg, Pennsylvania, something happened to change their comradeship to loathing.

Justice Department lawyer Phil Fox says: 'They had a real thing about each other – bad blood. But it's unlikely we'll ever know what happened to Hoffa.'

Phil Roemer, a former FBI agent who investigated the case, says: 'There doesn't seem to be much doubt that Tony Pro was one of the organizers.'

Says Mafia author Howard Abadinsky: 'Tony Pro knew Hoffa's fate, but the decision must have come from a much higher authority than him. He was just a soldier.'

Everybody knew that Jimmy Hoffa's disappearance was a Mafia hit but nobody could prove anything. Tony Pro continued to deny any involvement right to the end. Two years later he was convicted and given a life sentence for the murder of another Teamsters official. In 1988 he died in prison aged 71 – still denying any knowledge of Hoffa's 'hit'.

Mafia bigwig Russell Bufalino is reputed to have ordered Hoffa's death. The accepted theory is that the Cosa Nostra had such a good business siphoning off Teamsters' pension money and shaking down employers that they didn't want hardheaded Hoffa coming back and running it all. Fitzsimmons was far more accommodating.

A FAMILY AFFAIR?

Another name linked to Hoffa's disappearance was his own foster son …

An independent and reputable witness said he pulled up beside a brand new 197[illegible] maroon Mercury and for a few seconds saw what everyone believes was the abduction. He recognized Hoffa as one of four passengers. He was leaning forward shouting at the driver, and he had his hands behind his back, perhaps tied.

The witness identified the driver as heavy-set and swarthy, and picked him out of the mugshot book as Hoffa's own foster son, Charles L. 'Chuckie' O'Brien. Raised as a son by Hoffa, Chuckie had become his bodyguard and personal assistant. Now the key figure in the disappearance, he fiercely proclaimed his innocence.

The FBI did find the maroon Mercury and sniffer dogs picked up Hoffa's scent on the back seat and in the trunk.

So who abducted Jimmy Hoffa? And was he indeed murdered?

Just before he vanished, Hoffa had drawn a million dollars in cash, the FBI revealed. Also, twice in the year before his death he had sent emissaries to the Justice Department offering evidence that would criminally implicate his arch-rival Fitzsimmons. The department wasn't interested.

Fitzsimmons, his successor as boss of the Teamsters, was obviously a prime suspect, as the man who had most to gain by ordering Hoffa's liquidation. But lung cancer killed Fitzsimmons in the summer of 1981, thereby terminating his presidency and an enduring line of inquiry.

Or was the culprit the CIA? Through Hoffa, the agency had recruited Mafiosi Sam Giancana and John Roselli t[illegible] assassinate Cuba's Fidel Castro. Both Roselli and Giancana were later murdered and their killers never found.

Roselli had hinted in 1976 that he knew who had assassinated John F. Kennedy 13 years earlier. Soon after, his body (or more accurately, several pieces of it) were found floating off the Florida coast in a 55-gallon drum.

As memories faded, the investigation into the disappearance of James Hoffa seemed to be going cold. His wife died in 1980 after a long illness. His children, James P. Hoffa and Barbara Ann Crancer, continued their fight to force the FBI to release all information files.

In Hollywood's version of the affair, with Jack Nicholson in the title role of Hoffa, actor/director Danny DeVito gave a collection of possible explanations, yet chose none. The movie shed no new light on the Hoffa case and deliberately avoided making a definitive statement about his death.

THE END OF THE LINE

Then in August 1992, a hitman who claimed to have carried out nearly 100 murders came forward to say: 'I killed Jimmy Hoffa.'

The man appeared on nationwide TV in America, claiming to be dying from emphysema, and said he wanted to set the record straight. He took a lie detector test and explained how he took the contract to rub out Jimmy Hoffa. He told viewers:

'I was in Federal Prison in Atlanta, about to be paroled. A person from a known southern family contacted me and told me the contract would pay $25,000. This was too much money. Normal work was ten grand, that was the going rate, sometimes 15.

'I was flown to Detroit and taken to a junkyard. In the office there I met three men, one of them was known to me as Sally Bugs. As soon as I saw Jimmy Hoffa I knew who he was. He wasn't a tall man but he was well-built.

'Five of us including Jimmy got into a panelled truck. Sal drove and we took off. I didn't know where we were going because we were never told anything.

'We drove all the way from Detroit to Chicago's Lake Michigan. Jimmy was gagged with tape and they drugged him with a hypodermic to keep him quiet.'

Apparently, during the trip Hoffa recognized Sally Bugs as Salvatore Briguglio, a hood who would be killed a year later in New York's Little Italy while working for no less a character than 'Tony Pro' Provenzano.

The hitman continued: 'I've clipped people who'd beg and plead and say "take pity on my family" – that kinda thing. Not Jimmy Hoffa. He was a man's man. Tough as nails.

'Jimmy refused a shot of whisky, cursed at Sally Bugs and offered half a

Above: ***Hoffa helped to recruit Mafia gunmen to assassinate Cuban leader Fidel Castro, another shady link in the chain which bound him to his fate.***

SEVERAL PIECES OF THE BODY WERE FOUND FLOATING OFF THE COAST OF FLORIDA IN A 55-GALLON DRUM.

They dumped him over the side with lead weights taped to his legs. When the bubbles stopped coming up, they knew Hoffa was finished.

million dollars to call off the hit. It was refused of course. At that point I think he realized that this was the end of the line.

'As darkness came, we got into a yacht and motored to what looked like a Navy pier. Sal ordered us to strip Jimmy down naked. He never asked for mercy. I had to admire the guy for that.

'He wasn't afraid. He copped no pleas. He didn't beg for anything from us. Under the seat were these pigs of lead somewhat like what are used in a Linotype. They were taped with two-inch tape to each of his legs, to be used as weights, and he was dropped over the side.

'When the bubbles stopped coming up, we pulled up the anchor, started the motor and headed back to shore.'

Couldn't they just have shot him? The hitman told television viewers: 'One of the things a mechanic does is give the customer what he wants. That was the way the customer wanted it and this was the way it was done.'

Is that how Hoffa ended his days? The tiny man of gigantic presence had fought against the Mafia and for the Mafia. As leader of America's most powerful union, he ended up doing its bidding – and cheating on his millions of members. Yet the American people still find his story fascinating. This man who was a thorn in the side of authority remains in some quarters as much of a popular hero as he was in his heyday.

Meanwhile, the umpteen conflicting theories as to his fate are added to year by year. But there is still nothing concrete – not even a 'cement overcoat'.

Below: *Pickets from the Teamsters union demonstrate their loyalty to Hoffa, the man who pilfered their pension fund and plotted, even killed, in pursuit of power.*